VIVA! WOMEN'S LIB!

A Play for Women

by

STUART READY

SAMUEL   FRENCH

LONDON

NEW YORK   TORONTO   SYDNEY   HOLLYWOOD

MADE AND PRINTED IN GREAT BRITAIN BY
LATIMER TREND & COMPANY LTD PLYMOUTH
MADE IN ENGLAND

CHARACTERS

Nellie Erskine-Pym
the Prime Minister

Olga Pettingal
Minister for Foreign Affairs

Dora Teach
Chancellor of the Exchequer

Nessie Wittlesham
Minister for War

Babs Appleyard
Minister for Home Affairs

Gertrude Hammer
Minister for Labour

Valerie Cassel
Principal Private Secretary

Agatha Sykes
Commissioner of Police

Vicki
a film star

Mrs Lurch
a domestic

The action passes in the Cabinet Room at 10 Downing Street

ACT I	A morning in April
ACT II	Evening, about seven
ACT III	One hour later

Time - the very near future

VIVA! WOMEN'S LIB!

ACT I

The Cabinet Room at 10 Downing Street. A morning in April

A door in the centre of the back wall opens on to the hall, and another down one wall to the Prime Minister's private room. On the opposite side of the room to the private door is a large window

The room bears no resemblance to the Cabinet Room of the bad old days. Obviously the ladies have selected a more suitable apartment. The décor is gay and tasteful, chairs are comfortable and well-cushioned. There are flowers on the cabinets. The April sun streams in the window that overlooks Downing Street. The only austere note is a big table in the middle of the room

When the CURTAIN *rises, the room is empty. The radio is on with a girl singing a "Pop" song. Valerie Cassel comes in by the main door. She is a bright, attractive girl of something over twenty, well-dressed. She carries an armful of women's magazines. Humming to the tune, she deposits the magazines on the cabinet, takes copies of the agenda from the same cabinet and places them round the table. Mrs Wittlesham comes in by the main door. The Minister for War is a quiet, pleasant little woman of about forty-five. Her clothes are good and attractive, but, as always, they seem to suggest she is on her way to a wedding. She carries a number of parcels and an attractive carrier-bag*

Wittlesham (*brightly*) Good morning, Miss Cassel. (*She takes her parcels to the cabinet*)

Valerie (*turning*) Oh—just a minute. (*Switching the radio off*) Good morning, Mrs Wittlesham. Sorry I had the radio on. I didn't realize it was so near the time of the cabinet meeting.

Wittlesham You shouldn't have turned it off for me. It's "Men's Hour", isn't it?

Valerie (*returning to her task at the table*) Yes. They still go for the tunes with plenty of "love" in them.

Wittlesham Why not? We haven't abolished that, have we? But the poor men do have a pretty thin time of it these days. I don't know what my late husband would have thought.

Valerie They say the vast majority of husbands in the country have come to like it.

Wittlesham (*thoughtfully*) Yes; I think they do. And now they are relieved of the duties of national government it does give them more time for their own leisure—(*brightly*)—and to make more money for their wives.

Valerie And all done in six months!

Wittlesham (*nodding*) Six months. We've travelled a long way since Mrs Pankhurst tied herself to the railings.

Valerie Do you remember this room when we first took over?

Wittlesham (*amused*) Do I! The dreadful stuffy pictures and all that dark oak panelling. Now this is the kind of atmosphere to stimulate the brain. (*Going to the windows*) You know, I brought these curtains—and only ninety-five pence a yard. Which reminds me—I hope the meeting isn't going to last too long. I've got heaps of shopping to do.

Valerie (*glancing at the agenda*) Fairly heavy.

Wittlesham (*taking off her hat at the mirror over the radio*) Oh, dear. What's on?

Valerie Budget, principally. Miss Teach is still insisting on that tax on dart boards and billiard tables.

Wittlesham I don't believe it's wise. If men don't have a harmless outlet they'll grow restive.

Valerie (*reading*) New curtains for the House of Commons . . .

Wittlesham (*turning*) Ah, yes; I hope they'll leave that to me. I saw some lovely stuff in Regent Street—I know I'm Minister for War, but as there aren't any wars on, thank goodness, it gives me a bit of spare time.

Mrs Erskine-Pym comes in from the private door. The Prime Minister is a big, assertive woman of about fifty-five, with a worried, preoccupied manner. She is resplendent in an attractive housecoat

Valerie (*moving over to* L) Good morning, Madam Prime Minister.

Erskine-Pym What? Oh, yes; good morning. (*Going to the head of the table and glancing down at the agenda*) If you're here, Mrs Wittlesham, that means I'm late.

Wittlesham I'm not late, P.M. You've forgotten my daily woman doesn't come on Thursdays.

Erskine-Pym I've more to think about than your daily woman. You none of you seem to realize that most of the weight of this country falls on my shoulders.

Wittlesham (*going to her parcels on the cabinet*) We all have our responsibilities.

Erskine-Pym (*with a grunt*) Do you? Why weren't you at the reception given by the W.V.S. last night?

Wittlesham Oh—well, I had arranged a bridge four . . .

Erskine-Pym There you are. The country could totter to ruin for all you care. That sort of thing is no better than when we had men in power.

Wittlesham That's most unfair. After all, I did attend the dinner given by the Brigade of Guards.

Erskine-Pym No doubt you did. An all-men affair. And I bet you had a whale of a time.

Wittlesham (*examining some stockings she has purchased*) Not at all, I had a most exhausting evening. I danced with five colonels, eleven majors and platoons of lieutenants . . .

Erskine-Pym (*curtly*) I don't wish to discuss the details, Mrs Wittlesham. Only let me say that sometimes I think your loyalties are suspect.

Wittlesham Prime Minister!

Erskine-Pym The Minister for War should attend male functions merely as a figurehead and not as a Forces Favourite. (*Holding up her hand*) I don't want to hear any more. (*Running her hand along the table*) This hasn't been dusted this morning.

Valerie I'll tell the woman, Madam Prime Minister.

Erskine-Pym Yes, you'd better. (*Going to the private door*) Goodness, I must get changed; I'll have the whole Cabinet here.

Wittlesham I hope you withdraw your remarks about me, P.M.?

Erskine-Pym (*pausing at the door*) I do not. You're suspect. I made a great mistake in having widows in the Cabinet. They're always liable to slip.

Mrs Erskine-Pym exits to her room

Wittlesham Well! Now, isn't that unkind.

Valerie (*rearringing the papers disturbed by the P.M.*) She had a late night. Those W.V.S. affairs are always a bit of a rave-up.

Wittlesham I don't see why widows should be less loyal. And they are freer to concentrate on politics than married women.

Valerie I wouldn't know; I'm only a Private Secretary. (*Examining the engagement ring on her finger*) Still, I don't think one can leave men entirely out of one's life.

Wittlesham My dear, how could one? Not that she doesn't manage to get rid of her husband very effectively. Where is the poor creature now?

Valerie South America. She sent him on an expedition to examine frog life in the Amazon. As soon as he returns she's getting him into the next Everest assault.

Wittlesham (*picking up her bag and going to a chair*) If I were married to the P.M. I think I'd plump for the next Apollo blast-off. And see there wasn't enough fuel to get back.

Mrs Lurch, the cleaner, comes to the main door. She is a tough, wiry little woman of about fifty

Mrs Lurch You ring?

Valerie Oh, yes, Mrs Lurch. The Prime Minister is complaining the table is not dusted properly.

Mrs Lurch Not dusted? But I did it myself . . .

Valerie You'd better see to it at once.

Mrs Lurch Yes, miss.

Valerie goes to the cabinet and examines papers from a drawer, Mrs Wittlesham is sitting in an armchair, working on some crochet. Mrs Lurch takes a duster from her pocket and dusts the table. All the time she has one eye on Mrs Wittlesham and she edges nearer

Oh, isn't that pretty?

Wittlesham Do you like it?

Mrs Lurch Smashin' (*After fidgeting for a moment*) Er—excuse me—are you the Minister for War?

Wittlesham (*nodding, as she works*) I am.

Mrs Lurch Oh. You don't mind me askin', do you? Is there goin' to be a war?

Wittlesham Good gracious, no. With the women in power, I don't think any nation would dare to start one.

Mrs Lurch Thank you, miss.

Wittlesham Mrs.

Mrs Lurch Sorry. Only so many of the Cabinet are old tabbies.

Valerie Mrs Lurch, if you're quite finished.

Mrs Lurch Just comin'. Could I ask you a favour? It's about my boy Alf. Could you get 'im out o' the forces? I could do with 'im at 'ome. All this dustin'! D'ye know, when I've finished 'ere I've got to do the 'Ouse o' Lords. All them seats!

Wittlesham Oh dear.

Mrs Lurch I'm willing, but there's a limit. When there was a men's government they never worried what the place looked like. But now! I bet before I'm done I'll be dustin' the lions in Trafalgar Square.

Wittlesham I'll see what can be arranged. What is your son's name?

Mrs Lurch (*promptly*) Alfred Lurch, Private, Army Service Corps. Number two-five-six-four-five-six.

Wittlesham (*making a note*) Very well. I don't suppose the army would miss just one. I'll telephone his commanding officer after lunch.

Mrs Lurch Ta, ever so. Of course, if we do have a war, I'll let you 'ave 'im back.

Wittlesham We shan't have any wars, so don't you worry about it.

Mrs Lurch Ever so kind of you. (*She hurries to the main door*)

Voices are heard. Babs Appleyard and Dora Teach come in. Mrs Lurch goes out

Miss Appleyard, Home Secretary, is round about thirty-six, an ex-games mistress, jolly, breezy and full of vitality. Miss Teach, Chancellor of the Exchequer, is about forty-eight, tall, vinegary and dressed severely. She carries two bulging brief-cases. She sits at the table and unpacks these

Appleyard 'Morning, Witty.

Wittlesham Good morning, Miss Appleyard. And how are Home Affairs?

Appleyard Pretty middling. I've been able to dismiss half the police force since we started the Wives' Home Control League. The proper place for quiet discipline is in the home itself. And if it should lead to an occasional punch-up, better in the domestic kitchen than at the street corner.

Teach Huh! Have you told her about the demonstration threatened for this morning?

Appleyard (*rocking herself against the back of a chair at the table*) Oh, that! I should worry.

Wittlesham What demonstration is this?

Appleyard Don't suppose there's anything in it. Just a rumour that a mob of men propose a sit-in in Downing Street this morning.

Wittlesham Oh, dear. Does that mean I ought to mobilize?

Appleyard Bless you, no. Probably hippies and militant Civil Servants. I've had a word with the Commissioner of Police about it. If they mean business, I shall fetch out the Women's Judo Corps. That'll finish it.

Wittlesham I hope it doesn't come to that. They're always so rough.

Appleyard Of course they are. Five hundred ex-games mistresses from the best schools in the country. Oh. (*Turning to Valerie*) You'd better alert the hospitals.

Wittlesham But I thought everyone was so happy. What have they got to demonstrate about?

Appleyard (*pointing to Miss Teach*) Her. The men have got the idea the Chancellor has something pretty nifty cooking for them in those bags.

Teach (*grimly*) I have.

Wittlesham Oh, of course—the Budget.

Appleyard You said it. By tomorrow night half the public houses in England will have gone into full mourning. Old Teach is a bit of a stinker.

Mrs Erskine-Pym comes in from her room. She is now wearing an elegant morning frock

'Morning, P.M.

Erskine-Pym 'Morning, 'morning, 'morning. (*Going briskly to the head of the table and looking round in disapproval*) Is this a Cabinet meeting or some sub-committee?

Appleyard Hammer's always late on Mondays. She will do her own washing.

Wittlesham Seven children, you know.

Erskine-Pym That's no excuse. She should have a washing-machine.

Appleyard Says it's unproletarian.

Wittlesham I love your new dress, P.M.

Erskine-Pym (*pleased*) Like it? I've got a little woman who runs things up for me. Wasn't too sure about the skirt . . .

Appleyard I like it. Gives you something.

Erskine-Pym Does it? I want something that takes it off.

Wittlesham (*opening her bag*) Look—I've got a new paper pattern here . . .

Spreading the pattern on the table, she and Mrs Erskine-Pym examine it with great interest. Miss Teach flicks the pattern away as it covers her papers

Erskine-Pym H'm, cut on the cross. But I like the full bodice effect . . .

Wittlesham You can borrow it when I've finished with it. I'm working on a piece of slipper satin . . .

Gertrude Hammer comes to the main door. The Minister for Labour is about fifty, large and bellicose and uncompromising. She carries a shopping basket bulging with domestic goods, and a string-bag of vegetables

Mrs Hammer 'Morning, all.

Erskine-Pym (*turning for a moment*) You're late.

Hammer (*dumping her goods on the radio*) P'raps I am. I'm not lucky enough to have servants running round for me.

Teach (*looking up from her work*) I happen to be entirely without domestic help.

Hammer Maybe. But have you got seven children?

Teach Fortunately, no; I don't happen to be married.

Erskine-Pym Now, come along; we must get started.

Valerie pulls out the seat at the top of the table for the P.M. to sit. Miss Teach is already on her left. Mrs Wittlesham sits next to Miss Teach and Mrs Hammer at the bottom of the table. The only seats now unoccupied are the three on the downstage side. Valerie takes a notebook and sits in one of the armchairs. There is a buzz of conversation

Erskine-Pym (*rapping with her gavel*) If you please! May I remind you that all England is looking at us at this moment.

Wittlesham Oh, dear. Does that mean we are being televised? I wouldn't have worn this dress.

Erskine-Pym I mean that on the eve of our first Budget, the country is regarding us with considerable interest.

Teach They'll be put out of their misery tomorrow. (*Rising*) Now, I'll tell you what I propose . . .

Erskine-Pym Oh, no, you won't. We stick to the agenda, if you please. Miss Cassel.

Miss Teach sits

Valerie (*rising and reading from her notes*) Apologies for absence: The Minister for Agriculture asks to be excused as she is busy this morning on her fruit-bottling . . .

Erskine-Pym Well, really!

Hammer Not the first time neither. Missing every time she happens to pick up a couple of pounds of plums.

Erskine-Pym Circumstances not allowed. Next?

Valerie The First Lady of the Admiralty writes that she will be unable to attend any Cabinet meetings for a while, as she is having a baby.

Erskine-Pym Now, what are we going to do about that?

Appleyard I suggest there is nothing you can do about it. Just tell the navy to carry on.

Erskine-Pym I suppose so. But I must say that I am much perturbed at these instrusions of domestic life. The world must be peopled, but I should be better pleased if the supply did not come from the Cabinet.

Appleyard Hear, hear. One cannot serve man and the House of Commons. (*Brightly*) I say, that was rather good, wasn't it?

Erskine-Pym (*severely*) Order!

The main door is thrust open as Olga Pettingal makes an entry. The Minister for Foreign Affairs is an attractive widow of thirty. Most elegantly dressed, charming and sophisticated, she is the glamour girl of the Cabinet

(*Heavily*) Ah, the Minister for Foreign Affairs! How nice of you to look in.

Pettingal Sorry I'm late, everyone. I've done nothing since breakfast but charge round one embassy after another. And you know what it's like at the Russian Embassy. (*She puts her bag down on the telephone table*)

Hammer Since when has the Russian Ambassador been living at Selfridges?

Pettingal I disregard that remark. If every Government department was as well looked after as the Foreign Office . . .

Hammer Hark at her. Nothing but a round of pleasure.

Pettingal Conference after conference . . .

Teach (*acidly*) All scheduled, I notice, in places where the bathing is particularly good.

Appleyard (*nodding*) That's right, you know. Look at last winter—Cannes and the Bahamas.

Pettingal Are you going to tell me that in the bad old days Mr Heath was never called to the outposts of Empire?

Hammer Yes, but not in a sun-hat and a bikini.

Pettingal You stupid woman!

Hammer (*rising*) Oh, am I?

Erskine-Pym (*rapping on the table*) Order! Really, ladies. Please remember the dignity of your office.

Pettingal (*sulking*) If anyone thinks they can do my job better, let them have a try. Wearing myself out keeping the nations friendly—look at that dreadful evening I had with Communist China—eating rice with knitting needles.

Erskine-Pym Let us take the matter as closed . . .

Pettingal If you want my resignation, you can have it. I've got plenty to do.

Wittlesham (*rising*) Might I move, Madam Prime Minister, that we've perfect confidence in the Foreign Secretary . . .

Pettingal (*unappeased*) No, no, I am sure there are plenty better for the job.

Erskine-Pym Stop putting on an act! You are necessary to us. For the position of Foreign Minister it is essential to have a woman who is attractive—(*glancing at Mrs Pettingal*)—if a little over made-up—because of its influence on the men.

Pettingal Of course.

Erskine-Pym Then there's your name—Olga. The Russians like it, and that oils the wheels behind the Iron Curtain. We shouldn't do half as well with a Foreign Secretary named Kate or Maude.

Pettingal You certainly wouldn't. (*Looking round*) I take it then that the Cabinet has full confidence in me?

Hammer I keep my opinion to myself.

Erskine-Pym (*rapping the table*) Order, please. The matter is closed.

(*Rising*) I must remind you ladies that here, at the very nerve centre, we must have unity. Ours is a great responsibility, a sacred trust. For the first time in the history of our country women have accepted the reins of government. We have done much more than was ever dreamed of a few short years ago. But we must consolidate our gains. (*Thumping the table*) We must build for the future. Every day that passes, man, envious of our climb to power, seeks to topple us from our high office. Time is short . . .

Teach (*looking at her watch*) Yes, ten past eleven.

Erskine-Pym What? However, the agenda. (*She sits*)

Valerie rises and moves beside the P.M.

Valerie (*reading*) New curtains for the House of Commons.

There is a buzz of conversation. The P.M. raps for silence

Proposed by Mrs Wittlesham, Minister for War.

Wittlesham (*rising*) Now, my idea is . . .

Teach (*briskly*) Can't afford new curtains at the moment. Rigid economy in all departments is essential. Maybe by the time the next Budget . . .

Wittlesham Well, really! Just because the Chancellor chooses to be stinking mean it's no reason why appearances should be neglected.

Hammer What's the matter with the old curtains? Won't they wash?

Wittlesham They will not. Had it been a good washable material . . .

Hammer Send 'em round to my place. I'll have a go at 'em.

Pettingal A bit undignified, isn't it? Having the curtains from the Houses of Parliament bubbling about in Mrs Hammer's copper.

Hammer What's the matter with my copper? Seen many a day's honest washing, which is more than you've ever done.

Wittlesham Look—I've seen some good, serviceable material at one-fifty a yard. That's not going to hit the country very hard, is it?

Teach (*making rapid calculations*) Two hundred and forty windows each measuring . . .

Erskine-Pym (*rapping the table*) Matter of new curtains held in abeyance.

Wittlesham (*sitting*) Well!

Erskine-Pym Next item.

Valerie (*reading*) Report by Minister for Foreign Affairs on recruitment of personnel.

Erskine-Pym Mrs Pettingal.

Mrs Pettingal rises languidly and drapes herself

And make it snappy.

Pettingal Well, I don't know how you lot are getting on for staff, but in the Foreign Office we are seriously shorthanded. Since we came into power there has been a certain reluctance of parents to send their sons into the service. I propose to fill all vacancies with women.

Hammer Hear, hear.

Appleyard There are plenty of jobs left for men, but this is one requiring a woman's balance and intuition.

Pettingal I'm glad we're in agreement. In foreign affairs one deals mostly with men—and men are usually shaken rigid by a pretty face. I have found this particularly useful when negotiating with the French, the Italians and the Spanish.

Hammer I bet you have.

Erskine-Pym Well, what do you propose?

Pettingal A beauty competition. (*There is a murmur*) Winner to be "Miss Foreign Affairs" and all the runners-up to be drafted to embassies overseas. Brains may be taken into account, but mine is the one ministry where looks are essential. Last year we might have had a war with Spain but for my foresight in posting "Miss Blackpool" as Ambassador to Madrid.

Erskine-Pym H'm there's a lot in what you say, but don't overdo it. We don't want the entire Foreign Office run by the Toppers and the Young Generation.

Pettingal I think you may safely leave that to me.

Erskine-Pym Right. (*Looking round*) Agreed?

Wittlesham⎫
Appleyard ⎭ Agreed.

Hammer I'm not sure.

Teach Nor am I. To lay an emphasis upon physical attraction is to play into the hands of the men . . .

Hammer Or arms.

Erskine-Pym (*banging on the table*) Carried. Next?

Valerie Proposal by Minister for War for improvements in soldiers' uniforms.

Wittlesham (*rising*) Ah, yes.

Teach (*rising*) Madam Prime Minister, I object. I have important statements to make regarding the approaching Budget. Are we to fritter the time away on trivialities?

Pettingal (*rising*) And I object to the remark. I happen to be the minister who has kept the country at peace. That is rather more important than sitting at a desk doing sums.

Teach Sums! The prosperity of a country is its life blood . . .

The telephone rings. Valerie goes to answer it

Erskine-Pym Order! Sit down! Upon my word, ladies. This is Ten Downing Street, not Speakers' Corner. (*To Valerie*) Well, who is it?

Valerie The Leader of the Opposition.

Erskine-Pym Mr Cudlip?

Valerie He would like to speak to you.

Erskine-Pym Well, I don't know! The Leader of the Opposition to phone me in the middle of Cabinet business . . . (*Going to the phone*) He should not have been put through. Yes? . . . Yes, yes, I know you're Mr Cudlip. Well, what do you want? . . . What! My poor, dear little man, it is not the custom of the Prime Minister to answer telephone calls during a Cabinet meeting . . . Busy? Well, of course we're busy. We're likely to be busy for years and years, so go and take a long rest. (*Slamming the* *receiver down and returning*) Wants to talk about a scheme for a Coalition Government!

General amusement

Appleyard Of all the cheek. They see no hope of a General Election, so they hope to get in that way. What a hope!

Wittlesham Of course, it is quite an idea . . .

Teach

Hammer

Erskine-Pym } What!

Pettingal

Wittlesham (*in some confusion*) I—I mean it would be a good idea had we not already got a perfectly good women's government. Sort of— sort of might do another time.

Erskine-Pym (*severely*) I'm surprised at you, Mrs Wittlesham. Either we are in power or we are not. Any compromise with the men would mean a gradual infiltration by them and we should be back in square one.

Hammer She's a traitor, that's what she is. Ought to be chucked out. I know some places where she'd be liquidated for less than that.

Wittlesham (*meekly*) I'm awfully sorry . . .

Erskine-Pym Do I take it that you wish to resign your post?

Wittlesham (*in alarm*) Oh, no! I didn't intend any disloyalty. Besides, I like my job. Much more exciting than playing golf and bridge. (*Tearfully, getting out a handkerchief*) And I have done my best, really I have. All the soldiers like me . . .

Erskine-Pym All right. We'll accept the explanation and consider the matter closed.

Hammer (*leaning across the table*) But keep you under observation, see? I don't trust widows.

Pettingal Does that apply to me, Mrs Hammer?

Hammer You? There's no knowing what you get up to!

Erskine-Pym Order! Next item.

Valerie (*reading*) Training classes for men in domestic work.

Hammer (*rising promptly*) That's me. Compulsory service for all men between the ages of sixteen and sixty in household chores. I proposes . . .

Wittlesham (*rising*) Just a moment, please. You haven't even heard my proposition.

Hammer We've heard quite enough from you. Pay you to keep your mouth shut.

Wittlesham Don't be horrid. (*Unfolding a sheet of tissue paper*) Now, I have a scheme for improving the uniforms of soldiers. We want to get away from this awful khaki, so I have a pattern here for a pretty blouse effect——

Hammer (*shouting her down*) Training classes for men is what I proposes —washing-up, bedmaking, floor-polishing . . .

Wittlesham —an open-neck blouse in light blue or cream, made up in a serge material . . .

Erskine-Pym Stop it! And both go down to the bottom of the agenda.

The main door is pushed open as Mrs Lurch wheels in a tea-trolley

Mrs Lurch Elevenses!

There is a general exclamation of pleasure. Miss Appleyard pushes her chair back and goes over to examine contents of the trolley, which is by the telephone table

Valerie exits by the main door

Appleyard Any chocolate biscuits?
Mrs Lurch Yes, dear; I knows what you likes.

Appleyard takes a cup and biscuits and sits in an armchair. Pettingal takes a cup and stands by her. Wittlesham lights a cigarette and sits in an armchair Mrs Lurch wheels the trolley to the P.M., then down to Wittlesham. Teach waves Mrs Lurch away and concentrates hard on her work

Hammer (*intercepting the trolley*) Where d'ye get them biscuits?
Mrs Lurch Dunno. Come from the store.
Hammer (*turning to the others*) I know 'em. Thirty-five pence a pound. I could make better biscuits at half the price.
Erskine-Pym The biscuits come from the Ministry of Supply. I suggest you have enough to do without cooking for the Cabinet.
Hammer I have and all, but I don't like to see waste.
Mrs Lurch (*to the P.M.*) Well, what am I supposed to do?
Erskine-Pym Do as you're told. (*Rising*) Ah, yes, and concern yourself less about chocolate biscuits and more about your duties here. I'm not satisfied with the way this room is kept. Look at it! More like a factory canteen than the Cabinet Room.
Mrs Lurch If I'm not givin' satisfaction . . .
Erskine-Pym You most certainly are not. Look at this table. Hasn't seen polish for a month.
Mrs Lurch I did it this morning—honest.
Hammer What do you use?
Mrs Lurch Stuff they gives me. 'Ere . . . (*She gropes about under the telephone table and produces a tin of polish and a duster*)
Hammer (*going across to examine it*) That's no good.
Wittlesham I always use "Rubiton" at home. It gives a most wonderful shine to my piano.
Hammer "Rubiton", my foot. It's not what you use but how you does it. Elbow-grease, that's what you want. (*Undoing the tin*) I'll show you. Clear them papers out of the way.

The P.M. and Mrs Lurch gather up the papers and blotters. Mrs Hammer starts a vigorous cleaning of the table. Miss Teach clutches at her papers

Teach If you please!
Hammer Got the idea? Elbow-grease! There—see your face in it. Carry on rubbing while I have a go at the chairs.

Teach Madam Prime Minister, I object! How can I be expected to concentrate on a Budget in an atmosphere like this?

Erskine-Pym (*shrugging*) Well, it is the break. People can do as they like.

Valerie comes in by the main door

Appleyard (*stretching her arms*) Oh, for heaven's sake, Teach, do relax for five minutes.

Teach I really believe I'm the only one among you with any sense of duty.

Pettingal Teach can't forget she spent the first thirty years of her life selling stamps behind a post office counter.

Teach (*sourly*) Better get off, hadn't you, to your urgent business in Bond Street.

Valerie (*going to Mrs Erskine-Pym, who is finishing her coffee*) Madam Prime Minister, there is a woman asking to see you.

Erskine-Pym A what? Oh, good gracious. Surely you told her I am in the middle of a Cabinet meeting?

Valerie Oh, yes, I did. But aparently you made an appointment to see her here at eleven-fifteen. Her name is Delisle.

Erskine-Pym Delisle? D'ye know, I believe I did. An American. (*Rising*) This is all your fault. I expected the meeting to be over by then, but you all saunter in at any old time . . .

Pettigal I came as soon as I could. Can't do more. (*Looking round*) If there is any more coffee . . .

Erskine-Pym There isn't going to be any more coffee. We've wasted enough time as it is. The woman must wait. (*Rapping on the table*) Resume, please.

Wittlesham (*looking at her watch*) Well, I ought to go. I promised to look in at Wellington barracks for cocktails . . .

Teach I insist the Budget proposals are dealt with at once.

Erskine-Pym Oh, bother you and your Budget. (*Holding her head*) What a morning! If Gladstone ever had days like this, no wonder he said a few things in eighty-eight. (*Snatching the duster from Mrs Lurch*) You! Clear this picnic out of here at once.

Mrs Lurch Yes, m'm. (*She hurries round collecting cups*)

Erskine-Pym Cabinet meeting to be resumed at ten o'clock tomorrow morning.

Pettingal (*flicking over her diary*) Sorry, no good. Golf with the Chinese ambassador . . .

Hammer You can count me out. Told you I couldn't do Tuesdays—bread-making.

Wittlesham No good for me.

Erskine-Pym Well, you are a lot!

Appleyard Sorry, P.M., but you know we are all frightfully busy.

Teach (*rising and gathering papers into her brief-case*) Very well, now I know what to do. If you don't want to hear my Budget proposals, I shall go ahead on my own. And don't blame me if they pinch everyone. A fine parcel of women to govern. You couldn't run a beetle-drive!

Teach exits noisily

Mrs Lurch (*staring*) Well! 'Ark at 'er!
Erskine-Pym Outside, you! (*She bundles Mrs Lurch and the trolley towards the door*) Go about your business.

Mrs Lurch hurries out

Miss Teach is about right; a dangerous slackness has crept into the Cabinet. It's got to stop, or I warn you I shall be asking for a few resignations. In fact, there'll be such a rush on the Chiltern Hundreds they'll have to be rationed.
Pettingal (*using her powder compact*) Well, if you can find anyone to do my job better, I assure you I shan't mind a rest.
Erskine-Pym Oh, go and play golf with the Japanese ambassador.
Pettingal Chinese.
Erskine-Pym (*to Valerie*) All right, you can bring this woman in.

Valerie goes out

I shall require the Minister for Labour and the Home Secretary. I'm told it's their concern.
Hammer Not too long, mind. I've got a joint in the oven.
Erskine-Pym For all I care, you can have a joint up the chimney.

Mrs Wittlesham and Mrs Pettingal go to the main door

Wittlesham Well, bye-bye. See you all again soon.
Erskine-Pym (*sitting at the head of the table*) Good day!

Mrs Wittlesham and Mrs Pettingal go out laughing and chatting

Mrs Hammer takes her bags to an armchair and checks her purchases. Miss Appleyard sits on the arm of the other armchair swinging her legs

Erskine-Pym Mrs Hammer, may I remind you that this is the Cabinet Room and not Billingsgate Market.
Hammer (*replacing her goods in her basket*) Sorry, I'm sure.
Erskine-Pym (*staring at Appleyard*) Nor is it the Common Room at the High School.

Appleyard gets up

The woman who is coming is an American. We must give her a glowing picture of the only country in the world blessed by a woman's government.
Appleyard Okay. We shan't let you down.

Valerie ushers in Vicki Delisle

Valerie Miss Vicki Delisle.

Valerie goes out

Vicki, something around thirty, is a cutie, a glamour puss, and is dressed accordingly. At the same time, she is intelligent and a pretty good actress

Erskine Pym Be seated.

Vicki sits

You must excuse me but I am extremely busy. (*She puts on an act, going through a pile of papers with much rustling*) Argentina—Brazil—Costa Rica . . . (*Looking up*) Was that the telephone?

Hammer Didn't hear nothing.

Erskine-Pym You were always a trifle deaf. (*Going to the phone*) Yes? Yes? Oh, the Admiralty. Well, what's the matter? . . . I see, trouble in the Far East. Well, you'd better send a couple of aircraft-carriers—oh, and say four cruisers and half a dozen destroyers . . . Yes, big ones. That'll be all today, thanks. (*Hastily*) I mean, those are your orders. (*She replaces the receiver*)

Vicki My! You're sure tough!

Erskine-Pym I beg your pardon? (*She rings the bell at the door, then returns to her seat*) Oh, that. A common occurrence, I assure you. Now then. It is not the custom for the Prime Minister to interview just anyone at any old time of the day. However, as you are an American visitor, I make an exception.

Valerie comes in

Have a greetings telegram sent to Mr Kosygin. It's his birthday. And send President de Gaulle a "Get Well" card.

Valerie But he's dead.

Erskine-Pym Oh—pity. All right, forget it.

Valerie stands nonplussed

Hurry, girl, hurry.

Valerie exits

Now then, your business, and please make it brief.

Vicki Well, guess you know I'm Vicki Delisle.

Erskine-Pym Since you say so, I am bound to believe you. You bring a message from Mr Nixon?

Vicki Nixon? And me a Democrat? Look, I'm an actress.

Erskine-Pym (*staring*) Good gracious.

Appleyard If you'll allow me, P.M. I know all about this matter. Miss Delisle is an American actress . . .

Vicki (*incredulously*) Mean you've never seen me?

Erskine-Pym I have seen everyone from Marshal Tito to the Tribal Chief of the Bulawatti, but I seem to have missed you in the process. I hope your business is of state concern?

Vicki It sure is. Look, sister, your hairpin government has closed down my show.

Erskine-Pym (*helplessly*) What is she talking about?

Hammer The new Musical Comedy Act.

Appleyard You remember we passed a Bill forbidding all stage presentations of a frivolous nature.

Erskine-Pym Ah yes, so we did.

Appleyard As a matter of fact, it was I who introduced the Bill.

Vicki Yeah, I knew it was a slob like you all right. Home Secretary, eh? Interfering with the pleasures of the people.

Appleyard Rubbish. Now you listen to me. I know all about the affair. You opened in London last week in a musical comedy show called *Kick High*. As a result of the new law the production is off.

Vicki You're telling me it's off! I come six thousand miles to play lead in a sure-fire hit and it folds up after one week!

Hammer Quite right, too.

Vicki *Kick High* was a smash-hit! A sell-out—booked for months . . .

Erskine-Pym (*rising*) Miss Delisle, were it not for the fact that you are a visitor to our shores—an American cousin, so to speak—you would have to accept the matter like one of the general public. Things have changed in this country of ours.

Vicki They sure have!

Erskine-Pym The Government has been aware for some time that most of the entertainment presented to the public are of a frivolous, worthless and irresponsible nature. Useless in building up the mentality of a nation or of providing wholesome recreation for the workers. We will not have in our theatres spectacles designed to distract and undermine male audiences.

Hammer All made for a lot of goggling old men.

Appleyard And the name—*Kick High*. I ask you! What do men go to see?

Vicki They go to see me—kicking high.

Appleyard The Government is not against entertainment. Provided activities are confined to—well, an occasional jolly pantomime, Bernard Shaw or Shakespeare . . .

Vicki (*rising*) Shakespeare? Say, I sing and dance!

Appleyard (*sourly*) This is not a theatrical agency.

Vicki Well, I don't know. Listen here. You lot of tabs are going a bit too far. If you're not mighty careful you're going to stir up one heap of trouble.

Erskine-Pym I'm afraid, madam, that if you intend threats, you have come to the wrong place. Do you know where you are?

Vicki Do I? If you had a saucer of milk each, I'd say it was the Cat Show.

Erskine-Pym That concludes the interview. Good morning!

Vicki You wait a minute.

Erskine-Pym I said good morning.

Vicki Okay, Big Girl. (*Coolly*) Can't say I didn't warn you. If you took the trouble to look out of that window you might see a bit of a crowd.

Erskine-Pym That is nothing new to us. Downing Street is thronged every
   day.
Vicki Not like today it isn't. That crowd's come to see me.

Valerie comes in

Erskine-Pym Miss Cassell, have this woman shown out.

Crowd murmurs are heard from outside. Mrs Hammer goes to the windows

   And what is that noise?
Valerie There's a terrific crowd collecting . . .
Erskine-Pym Oh, good gracious, where are the police?
Valerie It appears to be something to do with Miss Delisle.
Vicki You can say that again. (*Going to the windows, she pushes Mrs
   Hammer out of the way and stands there waving. The noise off increases*)
   Hi, there!

*The noise of an approaching band is heard to mingle with the cheering.
Erskine-Pym and Appleyard go over to the windows. Vicki saunters up to
the mirror and stands arranging her hair*

Erskine-Pym There must be thousands!
Hammer And every one of 'em men.

*The main door bursts open and Agatha Sykes, the Commissioner of Police,
comes in. In uniform, she is about forty-five, tall and wiry. She is always
stiff as a ramrod, her speech is staccato, and all her movements have an
automatic precision*

Sykes (*saluting*) Reporting disturbance in Downing Street.

Vicki exits

Erskine-Pym (*heavily*) Our police are wonderful. What are you doing
   about it?
Sykes (*rigidly at attention*) Attempting control situation. All available
   personnel alerted. Demonstrators in large numbers approaching from
   direction of City, North London, Edgware Road, Clapham Common,
   Ealing Broadway . . .
Appleyard Stop talking like a bus-conductor and get cracking.
Sykes (*saluting*) Yes, m'm. (*Deflating*) What shall I do?
Appleyard Call out the Judo Corps. (*Moving to the phone*) And arrest that
   woman Delisle.
Sykes (*saluting*) Yes, m'm.

The noise outside increases

Hammer That's her—getting in a car!
Appleyard (*at the phone*) Home Secretary. Judo Corps in full strength will

proceed to Downing Street immediately. Fire Brigade, with hoses, proceed in the direction of . . .

Sykes (*promptly*) Edgware Road . . .

Appleyard Edgware Road.

Sykes Clapham Common . . .

Appleyard Clapham Common.

Sykes Ealing Broadway . . .

Appleyard Ealing . . . Here, you tell them!

Sykes takes the receiver. She stands at attention, her mouth moving as she gives directions. Erskine-Pym drops into a chair

Erskine-Pym What is all this? If it's supposed to be some incipient revolution it must be crushed at once. And do you mean to tell me it's all because of some actress?

Appleyard I'm told she is an extremely popular figure. What they term a pin-up girl.

Hammer Ought to be strung-up. If you ask me, the men are using her to stir up trouble. (*Turning to the P.M.*) Don't you weaken.

Erskine-Pym I have no intention of weakening. We run the country and we shall run it as we think fit.

Valerie (*at the window*) The crowd is moving away. I think they're following her car.

The noise of the crowd and the band dies away

Sykes (*going to Appleyard and saluting*) Directives issued. Available forces proceeding stations indicated.

Appleyard Good. Oh, relax, do.

Sykes salutes and stands rigidly at attention. Erskine-Pym rises and goes to the head of the table

Erskine-Pym A most frustrating morning. Unpunctuality, petty squabbles in the Cabinet, and now a childish attempt on the part of the male population to demonstrate their annoyance. It is fortunate we have a strong woman at the helm. Insubordination will be crushed utterly and completely. At last, after the oppression of centuries, woman has ascended to her rightful place not only in the home but as supreme ruler of the nation. Woman's hour has come . . . !

Mrs Wittlesham hurries in

(*Crossly*) Now what do you want?

Wittlesham The news! Have you heard it?

Erskine-Pym I've heard enough news in the last ten minutes.

Appleyard If you're referring to this ridiculous demonstration, that's been taken care of.

Wittlesham Oh, I don't mean all these crowds marching about. Something much worse, a real crisis.

Hammer The Russians?

Wittlesham No—worse.
Appleyard Floods, earthquake—famine?
Wittlesham No; oh, no.
Erskine-Pym Well, spit it out, you silly creature!
Wittlesham A strike—(*helplessly*)—of hairdressers!

There is a stunned silence. Erskine-Pym sinks slowly into her chair

From ten o'clock this morning every hairdresser, every beauty parlour in the country closed down. (*Slowly*) Just try and imagine what that will mean.

CURTAIN

ACT II

The same. Evening, about seven

The room is in much the same condition except that the table has been cleared of papers, etc.

Valerie opens the main door and ushers in Mrs Hammer. Their dresses are the same. Valerie switches on the lights and goes across to draw the window curtains

Hammer Who's she got with her?

Valerie She's dictating letters.

Hammer Hope she's dictating her resignation. (*Flopping down in the armchair*) Nobody could be more loyal than me, but if anyone ever made a muck of things . . . !

Valerie You mean this strike? Well, of course, people might say it's the fault of the Minister of Labour.

Hammer I don't want no cheek from you. I got more on my plate than a hairdressers' strike. Huh! Do you think I worry about hairdressers?

Valerie (*pointedly, as she comes away from the windows*) I'm sure you don't, Mrs Hammer.

Hammer What we want at the head of the Government is a really strong woman—bit of a dictator. See what I mean?

Valerie Oh, yes, I know whom you mean.

Hammer She ought to have been put out to grass months ago.

Olga Pettingal comes in by the main door. She is wearing a dazzling evening gown

Pettingal Oh, so you're here. (*To Valerie*) P.M. engaged?

Valerie Dictating, Mrs Pettingal.

Pettingal Well, I can only stay a few minutes. Seen the queues? There was one that stretched right along Bond Street and up Piccadilly. I left them drawing lots for the last shampoo and set before the shops packed up. (*Looking at herself in the mirror*) What do you think of my hair?

Hammer Looks like hair to me—if it's all your own.

Pettingal Had to have a go at it myself. (*Turning*) And, do you know, they're asking fifty pounds for a perm on the black market.

Hammer (*unimpressed*) You don't say.

Valerie Are you off to a reception, Mrs Pettingal?

Pettingal What? Oh, my dear, I'm due at four or five of them. I may just about manage the tail-end of the new film. I promised the Brazilian ambassador, but I'm not keen. Since we clamped down on light shows I shan't get much of a kick out of *Camp Life with the Brownies*.

Valerie I'll tell the Prime Minister you are here.

Valerie exits to the P.M.'s room

Hammer Nice little job you've picked up for yourself, haven't you? Seems to be all dinners and dances and gadding about with ambassadors. How would you like to be Minister for Labour?

Pettingal I should hate it. But what about this latest catastrophe? First the hairdressers' strike, now someone is holding up all supplies of cosmetics from the Continent. Think of that?

Hammer A cake of Lifebuoy is good enough for me.

Pettingal Oh, you only think of yourself. Imagine the women of the country without lipstick, face powder, cream! It's the most damaging blow ever struck us. And all because some man has got control of supplies!

Hammer I dare say my Shirley can help you out if you're short of a stick of *Kissproof*.

Pettingal What's the good of talking to you. As a matter of fact, I happen to be doing something about it. I have a contact abroad. That's what I've come to see the P.M. about.

Hammer Oh? Thought perhaps you'd come to borrow her powder-puff.

Pettingal (*excitedly*) I've found a woman who can beat the hold-up. If it goes through, we'll have streams of supplies coming through in a matter of days. Thank heaven there is one member of the Cabinet who is alive to the situation.

Valerie comes to the private door

Valerie The Prime Minister will see you now, ladies.

Hammer (*rising*) What sort of a mood is she in?

Valerie Not too good. She had a letter to say her husband is returning home.

The two officials exit to the P.M.'s room.

Valerie closes the door behind them and goes to the main door. As she reaches it Mrs Wittlesham comes in. She is in evening dress

Wittlesham Good evening, Miss Cassel. No one at home?

Valerie The Prime Minister is in her study interviewing the Minister for Labour and the Foreign Secretary.

Wittlesham Ah, yes, of course, all about this trouble. What times we live in.

Valerie I thought it was generally regarded as a very good time.

Wittlesham Oh, it's lovely having a woman's government, but the men are so spiteful, aren't they? If only they'd leave us alone.

Valerie But do women really want to be left alone?

Wittlesham Oh, my dear, naughty, naughty. You mustn't say things like that—it'll be taken as careless talk. You're engaged to be married, aren't you?

Valerie Yes, I am.

Wittlesham Well, then, you know it's your duty to the party to train your fiancé to accept the idea that things have changed. You must talk to him, and mould him. Men will never again be what they were.

Valerie I know. Makes it rather dull, doesn't it?

Wittlesham (*turning away somewhat evasively*) Don't ask me; I'm a widow. I think only about my work and my duty. I'm sure my poor late husband never thought that one day I should have the entire British Army under my thumb. (*Giggling*) Not that I know the difference between a tank and a sergeant-major. (*Going to the mirror*) I'm rather pleased with my hair—a home perm, you know. I must beat the strike, if only for the sake of the Brigade of Guards.

Valerie I'd better tell the Prime Minister you are here.

Wittlesham There's no hurry. I want to make a telephone call.

Valerie exits to the P.M.'s room

Mrs Wittlesham opens the main door to make sure no one is about, then hurries to the phone

(*On the phone*) Hullo. Give me Whitehall double-nine-double-nine-two. Please be quick. This is the Minister for War, and it's urgent . . . Yes, absolutely top priority—as high as you can get. (*As she waits she slips a mirror from her bag and examines her hair*) Hullo? (*Guardedly*) Who is that? . . . (*Changing tone*) Oh, it's you, Bambi! I thought I should have to get through a barrage of secretaries to reach you . . . Yes, yes, I'm in the Cabinet Room . . . I know it's risky, but never mind . . . Pictures? Yes, darling, I'd love to. All right, the Odeon in ten minutes. It's a film about the life of Mrs Pankhurst, but we needn't look at it, need we? . . . All right, 'til then. 'Bye! (*She replaces the receiver*)

Mrs Erskine-Pym enters. Mrs Hammer and Mrs Pettingal follow

Erskine-Pym Was that you on the phone?

Wittlesham Yes, I wanted to put a call through to Chelsea Barracks to see if they were all right for bugles.

Erskine-Pym Then kindly use the War Office or a telephone-box and not the Cabinet Room.

Wittlesham (*extracting her bag*) I'm sorry, I'm sure. There's your two-pence.

Erskine-Pym Oh, go away, go away. (*Sitting at the head of the table*) And sit down, everybody. Don't drape yourselves about.

Mrs Pettingal sits in an armchair, Mrs Wittlesham in a lower chair on the far side of the table, Mrs Hammer in the other armchair

Wittlesham (*sweetly*) Didn't you sleep very well, Prime Minister?

Erskine-Pym Sleep! With the burden of office crushing me down? Look at me! Six months ago I accepted this high trust with a fiery optimism and a clear vision. Now—(*banging her fist on the table*)—I am beset by difficulties—by pinpricks, ridiculous crises that ought never to have arisen. First this actress woman—she's stirred up trouble all over London —and now this strike . . .

Pettingal And that's not the end of the story . . .

Erskine-Pym (*glaring*) Are you telling it or am I? It's a fiendish plot, directed to hit where it will hurt. Twenty million women with straight hair and not a scrap of powder. That's what we shall be facing. Is that going to get us votes at the next election?

Wittlesham Oh, dear.

Erskine-Pym Now, no cosmetics. (*Turning to Mrs Wittlesham*) You hear that? A pretty sight you're going to look in a few weeks.

Hammer I bet it's all been organized by the Opposition. They would stoop at anything to get us out of office.

Wittlesham Oh, no; I don't think they would be so unkind.

Erskine-Pym You don't think! A great comfort, you are. Let me tell you, Mrs Wittlesham, that your loyalty is suspect.

Wittlesham Now, that's most unfair . . .

Erskine-Pym I don't trust widows—always got an eye open for the next capture. And you're no exception. Waiting to land a Major-General or some old Field-Marshal, aren't you? I'm thinking of having you transferred to a department where you can't do any harm.

Wittlesham (*in alarm*) Oh, no!

Erskine-Pym Postmistress-General. How would that suit you? You could muck about with the stamps to your heart's content.

Wittlesham (*with dignity*) I have nothing to say.

Erskine-Pym (*grimly*) You'd better not. Now then, where are we? We seem to live in a complete muddle these days. (*Catching sight of a letter in her hand*) And look at this. My husband writes to say he is coming home!

Wittlesham (*artfully*) Oh, how lovely for you.

Erskine-Pym (*fixing her*) You have a genius for saying the wrong thing. Coming home. Just when I get him fixed up in a nice little expedition to the lower reaches of the Amazon. Should have kept him completely occupied for two years at least. Fancy, a crisis and a man about the house!

Wittlesham Never mind. Think how lovely it will be cooking him a tasty supper instead of worrying so much about politics.

Erskine-Pym As far as you are concerned, this interview is concluded. You'd better get off to wherever you are going. And where might it be? Counting the sentry-boxes round Buckingham Palace? You busy little bee.

Miss Teach comes in by the main door. As usual she carries a bulging brief-case

Teach Good evening, good evening, good evening. (*Putting her case on the table*) Look, can I use this table? I want to spread my papers.

Erskine-Pym Everyone seems to come and use this room. Well, don't be long. I want to lay out some sewing on it after supper. It's just the right size.

Hammer Done the Budget?

Teach (*nodding*) I have. And what a Budget! Scraped the barrel.

Pettingal Well, what's up and what's down?

Teach Never you mind. But I'll tell you this. The only thing that'll be down will be the faces of most men when they hear it. I'm broadcasting on radio at nine o'clock tonight. You'd better listen in.

Erskine-Pym Don't you say too much. I know what you are. In the House of Commons tomorrow afternoon is the proper time.

Teach I know the duties of a Chancellor. (*Spreading out papers*) No looking.

Hammer (*anxiously*) Something off the breakfast table, eh?

Teach (*glancing up for a moment*) By the look of your figure, it would be as well if I took a good bit off the breakfast table.

Hammer We don't want no tax on soap powders; no, nor mops and pails.

Teach (*working busily*) We shall see, we shall see.

Wittlesham (*rising*) Well, I really must go. (*At the main door*) Don't be too rough on the army, Miss Teach.

Teach I'm not taxing the army. They've got enough to put up with in having you mixed up with them.

Erskine-Pym What have you done about income tax?

Mrs Wittlesham goes out.

Teach Up.

Erskine-Pym
Hammer   } Up!
Pettingal

Teach (*with a grin*) Don't worry. Bachelors—twenty to ninety pence in the pound.

Erskine-Pym That'll send 'em all rushing to get married.

Teach Not a hope. They won't be able to save up enough for the engagement ring.

Pettingal You are a stinker, Teach. (*Casually*) Hope you've gone easy with dress materials, jewellery and wines.

Teach (*returning her papers to her case*) Budget Day is tomorrow.

Pettingal Look here . . . !

Teach (*putting the case under her arm*) All the secrets are in here. (*Rising*) Still, I might just mention one or two of the new taxes.

Erskine-Pym New taxes?

Teach Pretty heavy ones, too. From tomorrow, special tax on all dartboards, billiard tables, pipes, footballs, cricket bats . . .

Pettingal (*in relief*) Well, that lets me out.

Hammer Pretty fair, I must say.

Teach We'll teach 'em to start strikes and disorders. Now, Prime Minister, I'd like to leave my papers where they will be safe until I require them tonight.

Erskine-Pym They'll be safe in that bureau. I'll keep the key.

Teach (*putting the case in a drawer of the cabinet*) Very kind of you, but I prefer it in my pocket. There! (*Rubbing her hands*) Well, I'm going to rest before I'm on the air tonight. (*Going to the main door*) I'll pick up my case on my way to Broadcasting House. Good evening.

With a brief nod Miss Teach goes quickly out

Pettingal Well, whatever the efforts to beat the bachelor tax, I bet they'll leave her out.

Erskine-Pym A real comfort. What I call a woman with a mission. I must see if I can think up some little gift for her in the Birthday Honours. Wonder if she's got an O.B.E.?

The telephone rings

(*Answering it*) Yes. All right, send her in. (*She replaces the receiver*) Appleyard. More trouble, I bet. Still, it was nice of her to phone instead of barging in like the rest of you.

Pettingal (*looking at her watch*) Might I mention that we haven't discussed this question of Madame Lamour?

Hammer Madame Who?

Erskine-Pym (*sinking wearily into a chair*) Who the dickens is Madame Lamour—some palmist?

Pettingal I told you; it's my contact over the cosmetic question. She came to see me at the Foreign Office. Why me, I don't know. I suppose because she happened to be French. Anyway, she is in the position to beat the Continental ban on the sale of cosmetics in this country.

Hammer Oh, is that all.

Pettingal It happens to be of vital importance. (*To the P.M.*) You know that.

Erskine-Pym Yes, yes; I know it. Can't say I have much time to powder my face these days, but it is the effect on the women of this country.

Pettingal Of course it is. Just imagine a few weeks from now. Women rising in the morning, lank hair . . .

Hammer What's the matter with paper screws?

Pettingal An empty pot of cream. Not a chance of a speck of powder, unless she rifles the Quaker Oats. No nails, no lips, no skin, no hair. What does she do?

Hammer Sends for the doctor.

Pettingal That, Madam Prime Minister, is the canker that will destroy us. A woman's power is in her looks, and that is what they are striking at.

Erskine-Pym All right, all right. Get the woman here and let's talk to her.

Miss Appleyard comes in by the main door

Well, what do you want?

Appleyard I'd love a cup of tea.

Erskine-Pym This is Ten Downing Street, not Lyons.

Appleyard I've had a simply frightful day. Half the police have been controlling the queues at the hairdressers. Of course, they're most of them shut now, but there's a few thousand women in Regent Street camping out with blankets and hot drinks in case the shops open suddenly.

Erskine-Pym Any demonstrations?

Appleyard Demonstrations! My dear, you should have heard them. One woman got hysterical and was dragged off to the police-station shouting, "Ted Heath and full perms!" I tell you, if we had an election now, the Liberal Party would look like a Cup Final crowd compared to us.

Erskine-Pym (*banging her fist on the table*) We've got to beat it somehow. (*To Mrs Pettingal*) Go on, get off, and let's see what we can get out of this woman.

Pettingal All right.

Pettingal exits by the main door

Appleyard (*leaning against the cabinet*) And this business of Vicki Delisle and her show is just as bad. Crowds of men parading the West End with banners saying "We Want Our Little Bit of Fun".

Hammer (*rising*) Let 'em parade. Too much time on their hands, that's what it is.

Appleyard (*scratching her head*) I don't know. Have we been too drastic over the entertainment question?

Erskine-Pym I don't see it. Plenty of good uplifting entertainment if one cares to look for it.

Appleyard M'm. Travel film at the Carlton, demonstration of Health and Beauty at the Albert Hall, Dagenham Girl Pipers at the Palladium. Can't go wild on that.

Hammer Looks like you're weakening, eh?

Appleyard Me? Golly, no. I'll fight to the last ditch. But who is behind it? Oh, men, of course; but the whole thing is too fiendishly intelligent for a man to have thought of it.

Erskine-Pym I believe the trouble is here—in this very place.

Hammer (*nodding*) I've always said it. Widows.

Appleyard You mean Wittlesham and Pettingal? Don't worry; I'm having them shadowed day and night. I'm expecting a report from the Commissioner of Police any moment.

The phone rings. The Prime Minister goes to it

Erskine-Pym (*at the phone*) Yes? . . . Yes, of course it's Ten Downing Street. Did you think it was Sainsbury's? Whom do you want? . . . Pussy? No, wrong number. (*She replaces the receiver absently, then reacts*) Pussy! (*To Appleyard*) Are you Pussy?

Appleyard Do I look like it?

Erskine-Pym A man distinctly asked for Pussy. (*Lifting the receiver*) Check that last call immediately. (*Replacing the receiver*) Now, what's this?

Hammer (*inspired*) Your private secretary.
Erskine-Pym I wonder? Engaged, isn't she? If it is . . . !
Hammer Always had my doubts about her. Too young.
Appleyard Doesn't have to be her. Might be any of us. Might be Mrs Hammer . . .
Hammer Look, if you think my old man would be allowed to ring me up with names like that . . . If you want to know, he's at home getting the supper ready and the kids bathed.
Erskine-Pym All right, relax. I think you're safe enough.
Hammer (*hardly mollified*) Thank you very much.

Valerie comes to the main door

Valerie The Commissioner of Police.

Agatha Sykes enters, salutes and stands stiffly at attention. Valerie goes out

Erskine-Pym Here we go. Parade of the tin soldiers.
Appleyard Well?
Sykes (*saluting*) Reporting procedure.
Appleyard I didn't think you'd come here to sing carols. Have you carried out your instructions regarding Mrs Pettingal and Mrs Wittlesham?
Sykes (*saluting*) Instructions implemented.
Appleyard Well, what about it?
Sykes Foreign Secretary—(*extracting a notebook and flicking it open*)—yesterday morning, rose ten-thirty—
Hammer Lazy cat.
Sykes —eleven-thirty cocktails with Wi Hi Loo—
Hammer Ah!
Appleyard Oh, that's all right; that's the Chinese ambassador.
Sykes —one o'clock, lunched at Ritz with Nato, Shaef, Unesco, Uno and Unra . . .
Hammer See! Five of 'em, and a shady lot, you bet.
Erskine-Pym (*wearily*) Will someone explain to her.
Sykes Seven o'clock, dinner at Dorchester, soup, turbot à la Maître d'hôtel, Chicken Maryland, asparagus . . .
Erskine-Pym *leaping up*) Yes, yes! Apple pie and custard. (*To Miss Appleyard*) For heaven's sake!
Appleyard (*tapping Sykes on the chest*) Look, we're not all that hungry. Did you or did you not find out anything suspicious about Mrs Pettingal?
Sykes (*saluting*) No report.
Hammer Well, what about the other one?

Sykes stands immobile

Erskine-Pym How do you wind it up?

Appleyard (*to Sykes*) Minister for War? And don't trouble to tell us what she had for breakfast.

Sykes (*jerking open her notebook*) Rose nine-thirty—

Hammer She'll have a breakdown.

Sykes —fed dog, cats, budgerigar. Arrived War Office eleven-five, left War Office eleven-ten. Lunch Savoy, soup, fish . . .

Appleyard (*warningly*) Ah-ha.

Sykes Afternoon, pictures, Plaza, seventy-five p seats, back row, held hands—

Hammer
Erskine-Pym ⎬ What!
Appleyard

Sykes (*carrying on bravely*) —held hands—

Appleyard Just a minute. If you're going to tell us she held hands with herself, you go down to the rank of sergeant.

Sykes —held hands, kissed . . .

Erskine-Pym Ah! now we're really getting somewhere! Who did she kiss?

Sykes (*quickly referring to her notebook*) Man, hat over eyes, collar turned up, dark glasses, big beard, walks with a stoop, buys ice-cream, two . . .

Erskine-Pym (*insisting*) Who was he?

Sykes No face, all hair . . .

Erskine-Pym Are we to believe that Mrs Wittlesham goes to the pictures with a travelling hearthrug?

Appleyard (*inspired*) Disguised! Don't you see? Someone Mrs Wittlesham is desperately anxious to conceal.

Erskine-Pym Conceal? I wonder she didn't smother the man. But where does it all get us? She's up to something, but what? And with whom?

Hammer Quite sufficient that she's going out with a man. I knew it! Always so meek and mild, I don't think. Go on, have her arrested.

Erskine-Pym Oh, don't be ridiculous; you can't arrest a Cabinet Minister just because she goes to the pictures. Come to that, there's no actual law against them having men friends. But holding hands and kissing . . .

Hammer (*significantly*) Ah. And say behind that beard is Kosygin and Mao?

Erskine-Pym Not both of them, surely. (*Pacing about*) But it's disturbing. (*Going up to Sykes*) Anything further?

Sykes (*jerking her book up*) Returned bed ten-thirty, hot-water bottle, Bournvita . . .

Erskine-Pym Stop! (*To Appleyard; grimly*) Get rid of it.

Appleyard Dismiss.

Sykes salutes and goes smartly out

Erskine-Pym For an official who spends so much time inside a person's private life, she seems to find out precious little.

Appleyard Sykes is a sticker. Slow but sure. She always gets her man.

Erskine-Pym (*unconvinced*) Does she? Probably come rushing in here with a handful of beards.

Valerie comes to the main door

Valerie The Foreign Secretary is here with Madame Lamour.
Erskine-Pym Ah, yes, the cosmetic contact. We'd better see her.

Valerie goes out

Mrs Erskine-Pym arranges her dress. Appleyard and Hammer move away, talking together

Now, what do we say to her? We don't want to appear too eager. If she thinks she's going to drive a hard bargain she's come to the wrong shop.
Hammer You be careful. Don't know who she is, do we? I'd be better keen on the idea if Pettingal hadn't thought of it.
Erskine-Pym Mrs Hammer, I will have solidarity in the Cabinet. If we don't pull together where are we? You're always suspicious of someone.
Hammer Widows will be our downfall, you mark my words. You and me's all right—the men in our family are safely out of the way.
Erskine-Pym Yours may be, but mine isn't. And I find it very disturbing. I thought Ernest would be perfectly happy paddling about in the Amazon for a couple of years. Now I suppose he won't want to go on the Everest expedition.
Appleyard (*smugly*) You should be like me; I've never given men a thought.
Erskine-Pym Nor them you, I bet.

Olga Pettingal and Madame Lamour come in by the main door. The latter is Vicki Delisle. She wears heavy dark glasses, a glamorous wig, and her whole appearance and manner is heavily "French"

Pettingal Well, here we are. Now, this is the Prime Minister.
Vicki (*languidly*) 'Ow do you do?
Pettingal The Home Secretary and the Minister for Labour.
Vicki 'Ow do you do?
Hammer Nicely, thanks.
Vicki (*going across to the window*) But 'ow wonderful! The seat of government! 'Ere we are at the very 'ub of things. An' see; the 'Ouses of Parliament, an' Westminster Abbey, an' Big Ben . . . !
Erskine-Pym (*to Pettingal*) Look, if she's come here for a sightseeing tour, we'll come back another time.
Pettingal Now, please, Madame Lamour, time is precious. We have invited you here on a matter of the utmost importance.
Vicki Ah, yes. Forgive, please. But your country, it is all so—so strange. I am bewildered by the noise, the crowds, the traffic . . .
Hammer Did you say you'd come here from France or from the Sahara Desert?
Vicki *Comment?*
Appleyard Better leave this to me. I speak the language pretty fluently.

Madame, avez-vous une petit pommade pour les dames?

Vicki *Mais oui.*

Appleyard *Très bon. Avez-vous la rouge pour la joue de la dame?*

Erskine-Pym (*impatiently*) Have you the pen of my giddy aunt! How long is this going on? If the woman doesn't speak English, there's nothing doing.

Appleyard (*shrugging her shoulders*) Sorry, I'm sure. Only trying to help you out of a hole.

Pettingal Madame Lamour speaks perfect English. Isn't that so, madame?

Vicki It sure is.

Pettingal And I have already given her a pretty good idea of our requirements. A large shipment of lipstick, face powder, nail varnish, mascara, rouge . . .

Erskine-Pym Can you do it?

Vicki But, of course. It is easy. I fill big sheep, she comes—*voilà!*—you are all beautiful. (*Pointing to Mrs Hammer*) Even she will be like 'Elen of Troy.

Hammer If you think you're doing this for my benefit, you're mistaken. Nature does for me.

Vicki Ah, 'ow true.

Erskine-Pym Let's get this straight. Since every manufacturer on the Continent is holding up shipments to Britain, how is it you are able to manage it?

Vicki Ah. The what you call Black Market. I 'ave my methods. (*Nodding slowly*) Our organization is ready day and night. When the word comes we strike swiftly. No one will know when the blow will fall.

Appleyard Are we talking about cosmetics or the first instalment of some serial?

Pettingal My dear, the French are always more highly coloured than we are, even with the make-up. All that matters is that she can deliver the goods.

Hammer How much is it going to cost?

Vicki *Comment?*

Appleyard *Quel argent . . . ?*

Erskine-Pym Cut it out! Now then, a shipload of cosmetics delivered within three days. Price to be arranged and no questions asked. Agreed?

Vicki *Parfaitement.*

Pettingal We've got to remember there may be a bit of an uproar if it leaks out. You follow me? Wild scenes at Southampton Docks as thousands of women storm the incoming vessel . . .

Appleyard Something in that. I will alert the police.

Pettingal You'll do nothing of the sort. We're not having Sykes trailing down every pot of cream that comes in. Oh, no, it needs subtlety. The ship comes in the usual way, then the goods are conveyed by road to a safe hiding-place.

Hammer Ah yes, but where?

Pettingal (*casually*) Well, my house would be pretty suitable. I have a large, roomy attic . . .

Hammer Oh, yes?

Erskine-Pym Oh, no. Just imagine you having the time of your life taking your pick.

Pettingal The idea never occurred to me.

Erskine-Pym Whether it did or not, it's right out. The goods will be stored —(*she moves about as she thinks*)—in the British Museum. That's safe enough. (*To Vicki*) How soon can you get the order through?

Vicki But at once. I go to my room. (*Dropping her voice*) In my little apartment in Soho I 'ave a radio set—'idden in the wash-basin. When it is dark I send out the message.

Hammer I don't like all this underground stuff. Playing with fire, that's what I calls it.

Pettingal Nonsense. A situation like this calls for a certain amount of risk. We've got to do something drastic. Every time I look at the morning paper I see disaster staring us in the face.

Hammer You mean every time you look in the mirror you see your face staring at you.

Pettingal One would expect a remark like that from a person who powders her face with Vim.

Erskine-Pym Now then, now then. All this petty squabbling. (*To Vicki*) You've got a ship, of course?

Vicki *Comment?*

Appleyard *Un bâteau?*

Vicki Ah, no. That I shall require from you.

Erskine-Pym You're a great help, aren't you? Ring up the First Lady of the Admiralty . . . No, that won't do—she's having a baby. (*To Vicki*) What sort of ship do you want?

Vicki Oh, a big sheep—very big.

Erskine-Pym (*heavily*) Would the Q.E.Two suit you, or shall we build you a larger one? We're in no hurry.

Vicki I think she would be big enough. Then, of course, it would be as well to 'ave a naval escort. Just in case of trouble.

Erskine-Pym Oh, sure, sure. And say a few tanks dotted round the harbour. And if you'd like Bomber Command to look in . . . ? I'd no idea the thing was going to be so easy. (*To Pettingal*) When you get your next idea, keep it to yourself.

Vicki I am so 'appy everything is concluded. Now I go to send out the message. In two, three days all your troubles will be at an end.

Erskine-Pym (*following Vicki and Pettingal to the main door*) I hope you're right.

Vicki (*unfastening her handbag*) Permit me to make to each of you a present. (*She puts two small packets on the table*)

Erskine-Pym What's this?

Hammer Time bombs, I bet.

Vicki A sample of our *Adoration* lipstick. Soon it will enlarge the smile of every woman in the country.

Hammer Not mine, it won't.

Pettingal Madame Lamour will now get to work, and in a few days time

this crisis will be over. I hope you'll bear in mind what I've done for you,
P.M. Birthday Honours and all that. I wouldn't mind the Garter, except
that blue isn't my favourite colour. I'll let you know.

Erskine-Pym Do. Let me have a list of what you're short of.

Vicki (*holding out her hand*) Bon soir, madame.

Erskine-Pym Good night. The Cabinet will now discuss your proposals.
I presume you are to be found in your hideout in Soho?

Vicki *Mais oui.* Three knocks on the door and ask for Annie. *Au revoir,
mesdames. Vive les femmes!*

Vicki goes out, followed by Mrs Pettingal.

Erskine-Pym Well, I suppose that gets us somewhere, but heaven knows
where!

Hammer I don't hold with it. I don't hold with it at all. Getting ourselves
mixed up with a lot of foreign spivs.

Appleyard Hammer's right; I think we've got to be careful. Pettingal
started it all, and for all we know she may be leading us into a booby
trap.

Erskine-Pym (*holding her head as she moves away*) Oh, I don't know.
What with one thing and another! (*Turning*) Did I promise her the
Q.E. Two or didn't I?

Hammer You did. And that's going to cost a pretty penny . . .

Erskine-Pym We should have found out more about her. We should have
examined her credentials.

Hammer If she's got any to examine.

Erskine-Pym (*with decision*) Have her followed.

Appleyard Right. (*Going to the phone*) Mind you, it's going to be tricky.
(*Into the phone*) Give me the Commissioner of Police at once.

The main door opens and Agatha stands there

Hammer You've got her.

Appleyard That's what I call efficiency.

Sykes (*saluting*) Reporting procedure . . .

Appleyard Yes, yes.

Sykes (*jerking out her notebook*) Concerning case Minister for War . . .

Appleyard Never mind the Minister for War. You tune in to me. Surround
Soho.

Sykes clicks to attention

Have the Secret Branch trail a woman known as Madame Lamour.
Deals in lipstick.

Erskine-Pym Wearing dark glasses and blonde wig.

Hammer Talks French. Flighty bit.

Erskine-Pym Knock three times and ask for Annie.

Appleyard Her destination will probably be the British Museum—

Erskine-Pym —or the Q.E. Two.

Appleyard Don't arouse her suspicions. Get everything you can about her and report back here.

Sykes salutes

Erskine-Pym I hope she knows what she's got to do.

Appleyard Don't worry; you can't teach her her job. All right?

Sykes (*at attention*) Surround Q.E. Two wearing dark glasses and blonde hair. Knock three times at the British Museum and ask for Annie . . .

Appleyard Get out!

Sykes salutes and goes

Goodness knows what she'll get up to with that lot.

Erskine-Pym Does it matter? I'm past caring. I'm going to try and relax over a good dinner. Then I'm coming back here to hear Teach's Budget Eve speech on the radio.

Appleyard Good idea, I'll join you at dinner. But I'm not eating much, because I'm on hockey training.

Erskine-Pym Unless you pay for it you won't be eating at all. How about you, Hammer?

Hammer I'm going home. Got a bit of hot-pot in the oven.

Valerie comes to the main door

Erskine-Pym We shall be back about nine.

Valerie Very good.

Erskine-Pym See what you can make of the letters in my room. They're in a frightful mess. I don't seem to get the time to be a proper Prime Minister.

Hammer Ah, does that mean you want to resign?

Erskine-Pym No, it doesn't.

Hammer, Appleyard and Erskine-Pym exit through the main door. Valerie glances round the room with a sigh, puts the chairs back in place, and exits to the P.M.'s room.

Vicki enters by the main door. Her movements are quick and surreptitious. Making sure no one is in the hall, she closes the door and examines the drawers of the filing cabinet. As she tries to open them, Valerie enters from the P.M.'s room

Valerie (*stopping short*) Well! Aren't you Madame Lamour?

Vicki (*dropping her guise*) Sure. I've been all sorts of things lately.

Valerie Well, I don't know. (*She moves towards the bell but Vicki stands in her way*)

Vicki Not thinking of being hasty, are you, kid?

Valerie I'm going to ring that bell and have you arrested.

Vicki I reckon you're not.

Valerie This is the Cabinet Room—strictly private. And I find you tampering with the drawers containing secret documents . . .

Vicki Ah, take it easy, baby. Sit down and let's talk it over.

Valerie (*staring*) You're not any Madame Lamour. You're that actress woman all the fuss is about.

Vicki (*nodding*) That's about it. Call me Vicki, and let's be buddies. Go on, sit down and relax.

Valerie moves away, considering her next move. Vicki removes her glasses and wig and sits on the edge of the table, shaking her hair out

Valerie You'll get two years at Holloway for this.

Vicki I'd rather have two years at the Palladium.

Valerie Look, I rather sympathize with you. I've never been in favour of what the Government has done about entertainment. But I've got to do my duty . . .

Vicki Sure you have. What does your boy-friend think about all this?

Valerie My—my boy-friend?

Vicki Ah-ha. Wear an engagement ring, don't you?

Valerie What of it? I'm getting married next month.

Vicki Do your bosses know that?

Valerie As a matter of fact, I haven't told them yet . . .

Vicki No. And what's going to happen when you do tell them? You'll be out, washed up. They won't stand for a confidential secretary who's a married woman, and you know it.

Valerie Maybe I do; but it's nothing to do with you. My duty . . .

Vicki Oh, your duty! (*Getting off the table*) You've got a new duty coming up. And what sort of a married life are you going to have with half your loyalties at home and the other half in this tabby circus?

Valerie I shall manage. It will be up to me to train my husband to accept the new state of affairs.

Vicki That's a giggle. If he's half the guy I think he is, he won't stand for it. So then where are you? Busted up. On the rocks. No good as a secretary, no good as a wife . . .

Valerie (*troubled*) Oh, no.

Vicki How are you going to spend your honeymoon? Sitting on the beach at Shanklin reading Hansard to him? He'll just love that.

Valerie We're not going to Shanklin. It'll probably be Torquay.

Vicki Not bad, not bad at all. But if it'd been me, I'd've settled for a Mediterranean cruise. Or, say a car trip through California. Sort of starts things off the right way.

Valerie (*shaking her head*) We couldn't afford either. And as we're saving up, we shan't have a car . . .

Vicki Guess I could rustle you up a Buick. And fix you up with hotels from Rhode Island to Los Angeles . . .

Valerie Are you trying to bribe me?

Vicki Wouldn't dream of such a thing. Guess I know how much this political life means to you. Oh, no; just trying to help you have a real good honeymoon.

Valerie goes up to the windows and looks out. Vicki glances at her watch

Valerie Mind you, I had thought of giving in my resignation . . .

Vicki Sure you had. You'll want all your time at home. (*Casually*) Got one yet?

Valerie We shall probably be living with Derek's mother.

Vicki That's great. You couldn't start housekeeping better. She'll be able to advise you, keep an eye on you . . .

Valerie I don't want anyone to keep an eye on me!

Vicki Oh, only for the first five or six years. You live with his mum, there's nothing like it. Of course, if you did have different ideas, I could put you in the way of a cute little flat in Sloane Street. Central-heating, icebox, luxury bathroom, super kitchen . . .

Valerie Please! What do I have to do to get all this? Shoot the Prime Minister?

Vicki Oh, no; that only leads to trouble. Besides, she's quite a nice old girl. Just leave me alone in here for half an hour.

Valerie Leave you alone? That means you're going to steal some secret documents, take photographs of plans . . .

Vicki The only photographs I'm interested in are of me starring in *Kick High*.

Valerie (*sitting on the table and swinging her leg*) Of course, if I thought you didn't mean any harm . . .

Vicki Harm? Just want to play a joke on someone. I can't resist a joke. That's why I keep coming in here dressed like a vaudeville act.

Valerie (*nodding slowly*) Well, that does make it rather different.

Vicki Sure. All you do is go home. You haven't seen me, I haven't seen you. (*Slipping a card from her handbag*) That's the address of the flat. Friend of mine—easy.

Valerie (*taking the card*) What about all those letters the P.M. expects me to send off?

Vicki Always tomorrow, isn't there? Guess you'll want to spend this evening talking over interior decorating with your new boss.

Valerie That would be rather nice. (*Going to the main door*) You'll see everything is locked up before you go, won't you?

Vicki Sure.

Valerie The cleaner will be in soon. I don't know what you're going to say to her.

Vicki Just leave that to me. Anything else?

Valerie (*at the door*) Yes, I'd like a couple of tickets for *Kick High* when it reopens.

Vicki They're yours.

Valerie goes out by the main door. Vicki goes to the mirror and replaces her wig. Then she does across to the other door and out.

The main door opens slowly and the head of Mrs Lurch peers round it. She is wearing her coat and hat. She tiptoes to the windows and draws the curtains. She has her back turned as Vicki comes back

Mrs Lurch 'Oo goes there!... Oh, it's you. (*She pulls out a chair from the table and drops into it*) I'm all of a doodah.

Vicki Better pull yourself together, Mrs—I'm relying on you.

Mrs Lurch (*holding her hand up*) All right, all right; give me a chance to get me breath. 'T'ain't every day I goes in for this sort o' thing. (*She rises*) I didn't never ought to be doin' it. I didn't never ought . . .

Vicki (*sharply*) You want to quit?

Mrs Lurch 'Oo said anythin' about quittin'? I said I'd 'elp you, but I 'as to wrestle with me conscience, see. Bitin' the 'and what's fed me, that's what I'm doin'. Goin' over to the enemy . . .

Vicki Okay, we'll call it off.

Mrs Lurch (*with alacrity*) Oh, no, you won't. I bin lookin' forward to this. Just me nerves, see. Look at that. (*Holding out her hand*) Got it proper, it 'as.

Vicki Then you'd better do something about it quick.

Mrs Lurch I will an' all. There's a drop o' somethin' in the cupboard next door. What the Prime Minister keeps for V.I.P.s.

Vicki You stay where you are. You've got to keep a cool head. Understand? She'll be here any minute.

Mrs Lurch 'Ow do you know?

Vicki Because I telephoned her saying the broadcast was to be an hour earlier. Any moment now she'll come in here for her papers.

Mrs Lurch All right, let 'er come. If it'd bin Mrs Wittlesham I wouldn't 'ave 'ad any 'and in this, but seein' it's that old skinflint . . . ! Let me 'ave just one good bash at 'er.

Vicki You can forget the rough stuff. It's all got to be friendly and good-humoured.

Mrs Lurch Pity. Look, if you wants to make 'er talk, I knows a bit of Chinese torture what might come in 'andy.

Vicki Chinese torture is out, and roasting over a slow fire. You know what you've got to do.

Mrs Lurch (*grudgingly*) All right, but it sounds a bit tame for 'er.

Vicki Get over to the door and listen. When you hear her coming up the stairs give the sign at once.

Mrs Lurch All right, I knows. (*Moving to the main door*) But I'd looked forward to a real bit o' "James Bond". (*Stopping and turning*) 'Ere, don't you double-cross me.

Vicki You'll get what you've been promised.

Mrs Lurch All of it, mind. Washing-machine, month's 'oliday at Blackpool...

Vicki Yeah, and a stick of rock. (*She goes to the P.M.'s door*)

Mrs Lurch New telly, twenty-three-inch—colour. . . . An' a crate o' Guinness . . .

Vicki Two crates!

Mrs Lurch That's all right, then, 'cos I didn't ought to be doin' this. (*She opens the door a little and listens*) Bill-O! She's comin'.

Vicki goes quickly into the P.M.'s room. Mrs Lurch moves to the windows and affects to be adjusting the curtains.

Miss Teach comes in by the main door. She wears a long outdoor coat and her usual hard and severe hat. She carries an empty brief-case

Teach Oh, it's you. (*Throwing her case on the table*) No one else here?

Mrs Lurch Not a soul. Everythin' as quiet as the grave.

Teach H'm, that's a pleasant change. (*Going to the cabinet, she unlocks the drawer and takes her papers out*) And don't think you're going to charge round here with a Hoover, because I've work to do.

Mrs Lurch I'm in no 'urry.

Teach (*sitting at the head of the table and spreading the papers*) You can go. I want a few quiet minutes with my notes before I go off to my broadcast.

Mrs Lurch Ah, going to broadcast, are you?

Teach I am. (*With a quick glance at her watch*) In just half an hour.

Mrs Lurch Well, I never. What are you—sort o' Jimmy Young?

Teach Stupid creature. When I speak tonight all England will be hanging on my words.

Mrs Lurch They'll be lucky.

Miss Teach looks up sharply

Teach (*with a sour smile*) Some will, some will not. If you have a husband you'd better keep him away from the radio. It may be too much for his heart.

Mrs Lurch Ah, goin' to bash the men, eh?

Teach That, Mrs Lurch, is a masterly understatement.

Mrs Lurch (*hovering by her*) Look, duck, get you a cup of tea?

Teach I am not usually addressed as duck, nor do I require a cup of tea.

Mrs Lurch Well, drop o' somethin'? Steady your nerves for your wireless act.

Teach Will you get it into your minute brain that I am the Chancellor of the Exchequer and not Cilla Black. And my nerves never require steadying.

Mrs Lurch Well, then, drop o' somethin' to celebrate? 'Ow's that?

Teach (*hesitating*) I don't approve of intoxicating liquors. However, as it is an occasion, I might have a small glass of sherry.

Mrs Lurch (*moving quickly to the P.M.'s door*) Comin' right up.

Teach (*glancing up*) In the Prime Minister's room?

Mrs Lurch (*at the door*) It's 'er sherry.

Teach In that case you can make it a large one.

Mrs Lurch goes off to the P.M.'s room

Miss Teach gathers the papers together and puts them in her case. She stands with her back to the cabinet, hands behind her back

(*Rehearsing*) Good evening. I am speaking to you tonight . . .

Mrs Lurch comes in with a glass of sherry

Thank you. (*Sniffing the wine*) H'm, the Prime Minister has an expensive taste. I must cut that down. (*Lifting the glass*) The Budget!

Mrs Lurch Bung-o.

Teach And confusion to all men. (*She drinks*) An excellent wine. Got something in it.

Mrs Lurch (*meaningly*) You bet it 'as.

Teach I have been in this room shall we say a quarter of an hour. During that time I have not observed you performing any of the duties for which you are paid forty pence an hour. Consequently your wages this week will suffer a deduction of—(*shaking her head doubtfully*)—a deduction of . . .

Mrs Lurch That's all right, duck.

Teach (*unsteadily*) And do not address me as . . .

Mrs Lurch (*coming closer*) No, duck. Better sit down, 'adn't you, duck?

Teach A deduc . . .

Mrs Lurch Let me 'elp you, duck.

Miss Teach reels forward. Mrs Lurch takes her by the arm and guides her to an armchair. Miss Teach's head drops forward.

Vicki enters from the P.M.'s room.

Vicki Well?

Mrs Lurch Okey-doke. She's gone for a Burton.

Vicki Into the other room with her. (*Together they support Miss Teach towards the P.M.'s door*) Find a suitable cupboard.

Mrs Lurch I'd rather pop 'er over the Embankment.

Mrs Lurch and Vicki go off to the P.M.'s room with Miss Teach. Mrs Lurch returns. She picks up the glass, replaces the chair at the top of the table.

Vicki comes in. She has discarded her wig and is wearing Miss Teach's coat, hat and horn-rimmed glasses. She picks up the brief-case and goes to the main door

Mrs Lurch (*waving her hand*) 'Ave a good time.

Vicki I'm going to have a whale of a time!

Vicki exits through the main door, as—

the CURTAIN *falls*

ACT III

The same. About one hour later

When the CURTAIN *rises, the room is empty. Miss Appleyard and Mrs Pettingal come in by the main door, switching on the lights*

Pettingal I'm sure I don't see the sense in coming here just for Teach's broadcast. Surely we could all hear it in our own homes?

Appleyard You know what the P.M. is. Says we should be together in case we have points in it to discuss. And you know what old Teach is. She may go too far.

Pettingal (*looking at her watch*) Oh, I suppose it won't take long to hear it, but I'm not stopping for any inquest.

Appleyard (*moving to one of the armchairs*) Bag the only armchairs while we've got the chance.

Pettingal Good idea. (*She sits in the other armchair, after pulling out a small chair for her feet*) Bad enough listening to Teach at any time without sitting on a hard chair as an additional penance. And I give her five minutes.

Appleyard Another wild night with the boys?

Pettingal Meeting the American ambassador at nine-thirty. Says he wants to visit the new night-club in Gower Street. Heaven knows why.

Appleyard But I distinctly remember we closed down all night clubs.

Pettingal You needn't worry about this one. Called *The Sewing Circle*. Closes at eleven sharp and nothing served except coffee and Ovaltine. The American ambassador is going to love it. Big spot is the Women's Institute Beat Group. Sometimes, Appleyard, I sigh for the good old bad old days.

Appleyard (*wagging a forefinger*) Now, now. Defeatist talk. Up the girls. We've all got to rally to the cause.

Pettingal Well, I ask you! Look at these strikes.

Appleyard (*hands behind her head, waggling her feet*) We shall beat them. If we'd been up against the men only the whole thing would have been over by now. It's the women traitors we are up against. Believe it or not, there are some who actually want the men back.

Pettingal Something in it, too. Women can control things just as effectively behind the scenes. The hand that rocks the cradle, you know.

Appleyard Can't see the application, particularly as some of us haven't any cradles to rock. Oh, no, we've got to the top and we stay there. I have no desire to sink back into private life.

Pettingal You please yourself; you were always so bouncingly militant. I'm not at all sure I shan't gracefully retire from politics. A nice little job would suit me—say a television personality.

Mrs Hammer comes in by the main door. She carries a large wrapped parcel

Here's Hammer with something tasty for breakfast. Anyway, she won't retire until she's dragged away bound and gagged.

Hammer (*putting her bundle on the table*) Just collected my blankets from the launderette. And what was that you were saying about me?

Pettingal Oh, just that you were the person who ought to be Prime Minister.

Hammer Were you? Then it's the most sensible thing you've said in months. I'd wake things up a bit. I wouldn't have all this weak-kneed wobbling. Clap 'em all in gaol, that's what I'd do.

Appleyard The prisons are already full to bursting point. Sykes made four thousand arrests between lunch and tea. As it is, I've had to give her permission to use the Albert Hall as a reserve prison.

Hammer (*sitting on the table*) Has she caught that actress woman yet?

Appleyard Not yet, but she will. Sykes stalks her prey, then pounces like a leopard. Anyway, she believes the woman Delisle has gone underground.

Pettingal Then it looks as if Sykes will have to turn into a ferret.

Hammer (*doubtfully*) H'm, she's not the only one to worry about. There's this Madame Whatsit, the face-powder queen. I don't trust her, I don't trust her.

Pettingal You never trust anyone except yourself.

Hammer Maybe not. It means I know where I stand. I'm surprised at the P.M. listening to a woman like that. Never saw anything so phoney in all my life.

Appleyard Don't forget Pettingal introduced her.

Hammer Huh! Anybody could take her in by promising her a box of make-up. It's time we started thinking less about our faces.

Pettingal My dear, I can understand your reluctance even to approach the subject.

Hammer (*getting off the table*) Here! What's that?

Pettingal Oh, go and count your cabbages. (*She kicks the small chair away and rises*) Look, isn't it about time we had a bit of comfort in this room? A chesterfield or a divan or two wouldn't strain the exchequer. About as cosy in here as a fishmonger's slab.

Mrs Erskine-Pym comes in by the main door

Erskine-Pym (*removing her hat at the mirror*) What's the time?

Appleyard Ten to nine. Teach will be on in ten minutes.

Erskine-Pym (*going to the top of the table*) Well, get yourselves sorted out. And don't think there's going to be cups of tea and cakes, because there isn't.

Hammer (*sitting on the left of the P.M.*) Is there any news?

Erskine-Pym There's too much news, that's the trouble. Things are going from bad to worse. Only three hairdressers in the whole of London opened today. How long will the women stand up against that?

Hammer (*leaning across the table*) I've got a scheme. Organize a home-perm corps, see? We operate from all labour exchanges. Every woman rationed to one hair-do a month . . .

Pettingal Wonderful. Before I'd have you messing about with my hair, I'd cut it off and wear a wig.

Hammer I thought you did. I bet most of what you carry about on your head comes out of a drawer.

Pettingal (*going to her*) What! At least I don't look like a dried-out mop!

Erskine-Pym (*thumping the table*) Stop it! Really! Just the very moment when we want unity and strength. How can I carry on with a Cabinet that conducts itself like a gang of teenagers?

Appleyard Chin up, P.M. We'll win through.

Erskine-Pym I hope you're right. Although exactly what we shall win through to is doubtful. Has anyone seen the evening papers?

Appleyard No; but I'm told there's a splendid photograph of you . . .

Erskine-Pym (*glaring*) If you think a cartoon showing me addressing the House of Commons in curl-papers is a photograph . . .

Appleyard Sorry, I'm sure.

Erskine-Pym That kind of thing can do damage. That is what is called the power of the Press. And they can do it because men control the Press . . .

Hammer Close down all newspapers. Allow nothing but *Nursing Mirror* and *Woman's Own* . . .

Erskine-Pym (*rising and going to her door*) I want constructive ideas, something that will make the men sit up and take notice.

Mrs Erskine-Pym exits to her room

Pettingal The only thing that will make a man sit up and take notice is a pretty face. What we want is a reshuffle in the Cabinet. Our strong hand is Glamour and we haven't even started to use it.

Appleyard I'm afraid I don't agree with you. That sort of thing throws us straight into the arms of the men.

Pettingal (*complacently*) What's the matter with that?

Mrs Erskine-Pym returns

Erskine-Pym Where's Miss Cassel?

Hammer Haven't seen her. (*She rises and strolls to the window*)

Erskine-Pym None of my letters has been sent off. What's she playing at?

Pettingal I expect she has a date.

Erskine-Pym She has no business to have a date. Urgent Cabinet communications just lying about on my desk as if they were so many football coupons.

Hammer (*turning*) What did I tell you? She's no good to us. Engaged to be married. That means she's thinking more about holding hands in the

pictures than typing letters. Dangerous. Almost as dangerous as widows.
Erskine-Pym All right, all right; don't you start on another widow hunt. We've got to have marriage and we've got to have widows. It's just that we haven't yet found a way of making them harmless.
Hammer (*grimly*) I have.
Pettingal Oh, you. You'd have the whole male population clanking about in chains.
Erskine-Pym (*looking at her watch*) Just on nine. Switch on that radio and let's hope Teach can give us a bit of uplift.

Appleyard goes to the radio set. Hammer hurries to take her vacated chair. Pettingal pulls the armchair up a little and sits

I suppose I sit on a hard chair?
Pettingal You're the hostess, dear.
Erskine-Pym Who would be a Prime Minister!

Mrs Erskine-Pym sits at the head of the table. Appleyard switches on, then squats on the floor in front of the window

Woman Radio Announcer . . . the position with the hairdressers' strike has rapidly worsened. A crowd of several thousand women attacked an establishment in Dover Street this evening, breaking the windows and making off with several dryers.
Pettingal Wish I had one.
Erskine-Pym S'sh!
Announcer With regard to the cosmetic shortage, a prominent doctor has warned women against the use of boot polish as a substitute for face cream. Neither, she states, can red paint be considered a suitable lipstick.
Hammer Huh!
Announcer By arrangement between the B.B.C. and the Chancellor of the Exchequer, the pre-Budget statement was broadcast one hour earlier than previously announced.
Erskine-Pym What?
Announcer The Chancellor, the Right Honourable Dora Teach, M.P., caused considerable surprise by stating that the time had come for women to recognize that men were their masters.
Erskine-Pym⎫
Appleyard ⎬Eh!
Hammer ⎭
Announcer She intended to repeal the present heavy taxes on the suffering male. In addition, an immediate bonus of one hundred pounds would be paid to all couples marrying by the first of June, this to be paid for by a suitable tax on spinsters.
Hammer (*rising*) She's gone nuts!
Announcer At the conclusion of her speech, in which she stated that the country would rejoice that men were coming into their own again, the Chancellor sang *Wave when you wish me goodbye* . . .
Erskine-Pym (*leaping up*) Turn it off!

Appleyard hurries over and switches off

Teach said that? Teach sang songs!

There is dead silence

Hammer Arrest her! Send her to the Tower!

Erskine-Pym I don't believe it. I don't believe it . . .

Appleyard Sabotage! If that was Teach, my name is Henry Cooper!

Pettingal You think it was a fake?

Appleyard Of course it was. (*Going to the phone*) The enemy has struck again.

Erskine-Pym It must be it! Get Teach out of the way . . .

Appleyard (*nodding*) Kidnapped her—impersonated her. (*Into the phone*) Send the Commissioner of Police to the Cabinet room at once! (*Replacing the receiver*) Fools the B.B.C. and does it all an hour earlier so that we shouldn't be able to stop it.

Hammer (*stuttering with rage*) Tax on spinsters? Hundred pound bonus . . . ? Call out the troops!

Erskine-Pym (*collapsing into her chair*) Oh, dry up. Now what do we do? All this will be in the papers, people will believe it. How are we going to explain it away?

Pettingal (*calmly*) You can't, so you'd better make the best of it. If she'd made it a thousand pounds, I wouldn't mind having another shot at marriage myself.

Hammer Traitor! (*Pointing at Pettingal*) She should be liquidated!

Erskine-Pym (*wearily*) Mrs Hammer, however strongly you may feel about this blow, this is not the French Revolution. (*Thumping the table*) Will everybody kindly keep calm! If we lose our tempers we might as well throw in the towel!

The phone rings

Now, who's this? (*Irritably*) Oh, go on, answer it, someone.

Appleyard (*at the phone*) Yes, yes, Cabinet Room . . . Who? No, Pussy isn't here. (*Replacing the receiver, then reacting*) What!

Pettingal. Who was that?

Appleyard That—that was the Leader of the Opposition!

Hammer And Pussy's one of us! (*They all look at one another*) Pussy is the serpent we've been nursing in our bosom. (*Ominously*) Who is it? Who is it!

Valerie comes in by the main door. She is attractively dressed for an evening engagement

Valerie Evening, all. (*She moves down*)

Erskine-Pym Ah, the Confidential Secretary. (*Jerking her head*) Watch that door.

Appleyard stands with her back to the main door. The P.M. follows Valerie

Going out with your boy-friend?

Valerie That's right. Celebrating.

Erskine-Pym Very nice. Very, very nice. I knew it was something important when I saw my letters in the other room.

Valerie Oh, those. Sorry, 'fraid I'm a bit too busy.

Hammer (*insidiously*) This boy-friend of yours—in a big way of business, isn't he?

Valerie Not so bad. But he was a bit messed up by some army service.

Hammer Army service? (*Insinuating*) What—Mr Cudlip?

Valerie (*staring*) Who?

Pettingal Look, if Mr Cudlip had any army service it would be something in the Crimea. It isn't her.

Valerie (*with a shrug*) I don't know what you're all talking about. I merely popped in to give you my resignation. And I can't hang about, because Derek and I are having a little dinner.

Erskine-Pym Having a little dinner, are you? And going to hand in your resignation, are you? We'll see about that!

Valerie You can't stop me. Mind you, I should like to have helped you out, seeing the mess you are in. But when one has things more important to attend to . . .

Appleyard Such as?

Valerie I'm getting married. I shall have simply heaps to get ready. Of course, it was quite fun playing about with politics, but now that it's obvious the women have had it . . .

Hammer Had it, have we?

Valerie Good lord, yes; plain as the nose on your face. If you take my advice, you'll settle for a coalition. And be lucky to get away with it. Oh, I still think women have a great part to play, but with men, not against them.

Hammer Will you listen to her!

Appleyard She can't get away with that, you know.

Erskine-Pym (*returning to the top of the table*) She's not going to get away with it. She can't just walk out of a Cabinet appointment as though it were a job at the local grocers.

Sykes comes in by the main door

Arrest that woman!

Sykes salutes. She goes to Miss Appleyard and claps her on the shoulder

Sykes I arrest you in the name of the law.

Appleyard Not me, you idiot. (*Pointing to Valerie*) Her!

Sykes (*repeating the action with Valerie*) Anything you say may be taken down and . . .

Valerie (*shrugging her shoulders*) Okay. But you'll be sorry for it.

Sykes (*saluting*) Permission to use adjoining room as temporary gaol.

Erskine-Pym What, my office?

Sykes All substitute prisons now full, including Harrods' Stores, Wembley Stadium, Festival Hall . . .

Appleyard Better in your office than have your personal private secretary carted off to Bow Street in a Black Maria.

Erskine-Pym (*resignedly*) Oh, do as you like. And if you want my bedroom as well, just let me know.

Sykes 'Shun! Left turn. For-ward! (*She gives Valerie a push*)

Valerie and Sykes exit to the P.M.'s room

Pettingal All this is giving Sykes the time of her life, but it's not helping the situation one little bit. Far more sensible if you'd sent her looking for Teach.

Erskine-Pym Oh, I'd forgotten about her.

Pettingal For all we know, she may be tied to the Tower Bridge with the water lapping her chin.

Hammer If she was kidnapped. But was she? How do we know?

Sykes enters carrying a large black beard

Sykes (*saluting*) Reporting procedure . . .

Pettingal Here we go again.

Erskine-Pym I don't mind you using my room, but I won't have you taking the stuffing out of my cushions.

Sykes places the beard on the table and stands to attention

Sykes Exhibit A.

Hammer Looks like a false beard.

Appleyard What did you think it was—seaweed? Where did you get this?

Sykes Removed from face of man accompanying Minister for War from Savoy Hotel . . .

Pettingal Might have been more useful if you'd brought the face and left the beard behind.

Sykes Struggle ensued, suspect evaded capture, dodged into green-grocer's shop . . .

Erskine-Pym Where I suppose he disguised himself as a cauliflower.

Sykes Photograph of suspect secured by nearby press photographer. (*Placing a photo on the table*) Exhibit B.

Erskine-Pym (*wearily*) I'll buy it. (*She looks at the photo, then leaps to her feet*) What's this! You're sure this was the person with Mrs Wittlesham?

Sykes Accredited witnesses at scene of incident . . .

Hammer Well, who is it?

Erskine-Pym Mr Cudlip, the Leader of the Opposition!

There is a stunned silence. Then Appleyard and Hammer each grab the photo and look at it

Pettingal Well, what do you know!

Erskine-Pym Our Minister for War is carrying on with the Leader of the Opposition!

Appleyard Arrest her immediately!

Sykes salutes and goes off by the main door

Hammer Goes to the pictures with him, goes out to dinner with him. Flirting with the enemy! That's treason, that's . . .

Erskine-Pym Oh, belt up. We know what it is, but what are we going to do about it?

Pettingal What can you do? Is it a crime?

Hammer It's the most horrible crime you could think of. It's a betrayal of high Government office! It's, it's . . . Oh, if only we could go back a few hundred years, she wouldn't have to worry about home-perms!

Appleyard We'd better send for the Attorney-General and find out the legal position.

Pettingal What's the good of her? She'll talk for hours.

Erskine-Pym But we've got to know if flirting with the enemy is a punishable offence. (*Going to the cabinet and pulling out drawers at random*) What's her number?

Pettingal Better ask your secretary.

Erskine-Pym Suppose I had. (*Going to the door of her room, then stopping short*) We've just locked her up. We can't discuss office routine with a prisoner.

Appleyard The situation is sufficiently serious to waive that. (*She opens the door*) Prisoner, forward!

Valerie comes to the door with a notebook in her hand

You are required to give the telephone number of the Attorney-General.

Valerie Sorry, I don't work here any more.

Hammer None of your lip.

Valerie What do you want it for?

Erskine-Pym We require to know if we are legally correct in arresting the Minister for War for flirting with the Opposition.

Valerie I shouldn't advise it. Mrs Wittlesham may look a quiet little thing, but she's a devil when she's roused. Anyway, you'll find the number filed away somewhere.

Erskine-Pym (*in exasperation*) Oh! And what's that you've got there?

Valerie Just private stuff.

Hammer Something in code, eh? Plans to overthrow the Government . . .

Valerie Well, actually, it's my wedding present list. I don't know how you lot feel about it now we've split up, but I could do with a canteen of cutlery, coloured sheets, set of saucepans . . .

Erskine-Pym Take her away!

Appleyard Inside, you. (*She thrusts Valerie back into the P.M.'s room and closes the door*)

Erskine-Pym Who would be a Prime Minister? Frustrated at every turn.

Appleyard Steady the Buffs. It won't help if we panic. Personally I always rise to the occasion when there is a crisis. Gives me something to get my teeth into.

Hammer Then stick 'em in Wittlesham, and bite hard.

Pettingal Things seem to be going wrong all round, don't they? Mind you, I don't believe Mrs Wittlesham organized these strikes. But what if Cudlip put her up to it?

Erskine-Pym We don't know, we don't know. But to have a Cabinet Minister holding hands at the cinema with my opposite number . . . !

Pettingal Well, you didn't give him the chance to hold hands with you.

Erskine-Pym (*glaring at her*) Mrs Pettingal, this is no time to be facetious. As a matter of fact, I've noticed you seem to regard the whole thing as rather amusing. Don't you?

Pettingal Oh, hardly that. I don't want the men to do us down. After all, I am a woman.

Hammer You're a widow, and that's the most dangerous type—a woman without a man.

Pettingal Not so you'd notice. (*Going to the main door*) I think my job is to go round the embassies and see what the reaction is to Teach's speech. All right, P.M.?

Erskine-Pym Do what you like; you're not much good here. And if you hurry you might be in time for coffee and biscuits.

Pettingal goes out by the main door

Now then. We now know who Pussy is. Are we going to say nothing and let her hang herself?

Hammer If there's any hanging to be done . . .

Appleyard That's it. Lead her up the garden, see? Who knows what unlikely people it's going to show up.

Hammer Like Mrs Pettingal.

Sykes comes in from the main door and stands stiffly

Erskine-Pym You know, I dread seeing this woman. Have you come to say anything or just fill up space?

Sykes (*saluting*) Reporting . . .

Erskine-Pym We know. We didn't think you were going to strip-tease.

Sykes Suspected person found lurking in basement of building . . .

Appleyard What building?

Sykes Number Ten Downing Street . . .

Hammer Send round there.

Erskine-Pym That's here. You mean to say there's Guy Fawkes stuff going on in the cellars?

Sykes Person apprehended and taken into custody. Interrogated, murmured suspicious words . . .

Appleyard Who is it?

Sykes Female, domestic, slightly inebriated . . .

Hammer But what did she say?

Sykes (*flicking open her notebook*) "Crate of Guinness, twenty-three-inch telly, stick of rock . . ."

Erskine-Pym We're not interested in somebody's shopping list. Did she say anything vital?

Sykes (*referring to her notebook*) "Old Teach has gone for a Burton."

Appleyard Ridiculous. Teach is a teetotaller.

Erskine-Pym Oh, bring her in. Might as well see if there's anything in it.

Sykes salutes and goes out by the main door. Her voice is heard off: "Prisoner, forward!"

This woman Sykes seems to suck up trouble like a vacuum-cleaner.

Mrs Lurch enters furtively. She is wearing her hat and coat. Sykes follows

Appleyard It's Mrs Lurch.

Mrs Lurch All right, it's a cop.

Appleyard What have you been up to?

Mrs Lurch Ah, like to know, wouldn't you? But me lips is sealed. (*Flopping into a chair, where she proceeds to put on a "Secret Agent" act*) Go on, grill me.

Erskine-Pym My good woman, this is not a restaurant. And I'm not interested in you grilled, fried or boiled. What are you doing on Government premises at this hour of night?

Mrs Lurch I won't speak.

There is a silence. The others look at one another

I said I won't speak. Me country is at stake. Do your worst.

Hammer She's had a drop too much.

Appleyard Leave this to me. (*Going to Mrs Lurch*) What exactly did you mean by the words "Old Teach has gone for a Burton?"

Mrs Lurch shuts her mouth tightly

Answer, will you!

Mrs Lurch Ah, that's more like it. Now, if you've got a red 'ot poker you could start 'eatin' up . . . Then you wants some lights glarin' down on me so's I can't sleep . . .

Erskine-Pym Sleep?

Mrs Lurch An' music what goes on an' on . . .

Erskine-Pym Quite sure there's nothing else you can think of?

Sykes (*laying a hand on Mrs Lurch's shoulder*) Permission to remove prisoner.

Mrs Lurch (*getting up*) Keep your 'ands off me, 'Immler. You an' your blood'ounds 'ave done their dirty work, but I'm a British citizen, see? I've struck a blow for freedom. An' me friends is waitin' to revenge me. In the years to come me name will go down to posterior. (*Dramatically*) I'm ready to face whatever 'ell you've got waitin' for me.

Hammer What do we do about this?

Erskine-Pym Only one thing we can do.

Appleyard Right. She's asked for it, now she's going to get it.
Mrs Lurch (*bracing herself, eyes shut*) Tell me the worst. I can take it.
Appleyard Collect your insurance cards and hop it.
Mrs Lurch (*deflating*) Insurance cards?

There is sudden banging at the door to the P.M.'s room. Sykes throws the door open. Miss Teach staggers into the room. She is wearing Vicki's coat and wig

Hammer It's that Lamour woman.
Appleyard It's not, it's Teach.
Erskine-Pym Teach!

Miss Teach sinks into an armchair

What do you mean by coming here disguised?
Teach Disguised! Do you know what's happened to me?
Appleyard No idea, unless you're supposed to be "Miss Income Tax Nineteen-seventy-three".
Teach (*almost inarticulate with rage*) I've been drugged, bundled into a cupboard—locked up for two hours!
Appleyard Locked up?
Teach Locked up. I might have been there for weeks if Miss Cassel hadn't heard me banging.
Erskine-Pym So that's it! And in the meantime someone has impersonated you and delivered the most frightful speech over the radio.
Hammer Who done it? Who done it?
Teach (*catching sight of Mrs Lurch*) She done it! I mean, did it. (*Rising*) That is the woman who drugged me!
Mrs Lurch (*all smiles*) Now this is something like. I done it all right.
Erskine-Pym You mean to say your went to Broadcasting House and talked all that distorted nonsense . . . ?
Mrs Lurch Well, I wouldn't go as far as that. But I'm the master criminal, see? I'm known as the 'ooded 'orror of Whitehall.
Appleyard Rubbish. She's just a cat's-paw.
Mrs Lurch Don't you call me names.
Appleyard She let someone in when the house was empty. Between them they bundled old Teach into the cupboard in the P.M.'s room. Take her away.

Sykes takes a step forward

Mrs Lurch Ah! the Tower at last.
Sykes Left turn. For-ward!
Mrs Lurch 'Ands off, flattie. (*She goes with dignity towards the P.M.'s room*) It's a far far better thing what I does now than what I ever done . . .

Sykes pushes Mrs Lurch into the P.M.'s room then closes the door and stands with her back to it

Erskine-Pym Now what do we do?

Appleyard First of all, give Teach a haircut. It's bad enough looking at her face when it's normal.

Teach (*dragging off the wig and going across to the P.M.*) My speech!

Erskine-Pym Oh, your speech. You've had it. Tax on spinsters, eh? Man coming into his own again. We're in a nice old mess.

Hammer But who was it spoke on the radio in her place?

Erskine-Pym Don't ask me. Everything is collapsing around us.

Appleyard I say, we're frightful idiots. Of course we know who it was.

Erskine-Pym (*wearily*) Do we?

Appleyard That Lamour woman! How else could Teach be wearing her wig?

Hammer And if Lamour wears a wig, who is underneath?

Appleyard (*thinking it out*) Vicki Delisle! The actress, the one who started all the trouble.

Erskine-Pym That's it! Declare a State of Emergency.

Appleyard hurries to the phone

Call out the troops. Proclaim Martial Law!

Hammer Don't forget it was Mrs Pettingal brought that woman up here.

Erskine-Pym Arrest the Foreign Secretary!

Appleyard (*at the phone; rapidly*) War Office, Home Office, Police—

Erskine-Pym Ring the church bells!

Appleyard (*into the phone*) —Archbishop of Canterbury . . .

Mrs Pettingal comes in from the main door

Pettingal I've got a few reactions to the Budget speech. D'ye know, they've started to form queues at the register offices already. And for the rest of it, everybody seems to think it rather funny.

Erskine-Pym (*ominously*) Oh, do they?

Pettingal Well, I ask you. The idea of old Teach turning into a woman-hater . . .

Teach What's that about old Teach?

Erskine-Pym Officer, do your duty.

Sykes (*going to Mrs Pettingal*) I arrest you in the name of the law.

Pettingal Oh, run away and play games.

Sykes I must warn you, anything you say . . .

Pettingal (*looking at the others*) What sort of a joke is this?

Appleyard No joke at all. You are a suspected person. In fact, there happens to be hardly anybody left who isn't a suspected person.

Pettigal No? (*With a laugh*) Well, I take off my hat to her. Madame Lamour?

Hammer Introduced that scent woman to us, didn't you? She happens to be none other than that music-hall creature.

Pettingal What a giggle. I certainly take my hat off . . .

Hammer (*to Sykes*) Take her away. And take off her head!

Sykes (*turning to Appleyard*) Instructions regarding decapitation . . .

Appleyard Relax. Take her away. And when you've locked her up, surround Downing Street with the Judo Corps.

Sykes (*saluting*) For-ward—march!

Pettingal Oh, go back to the Brownies. (*Taking out her powder compact*)
I've never marched anywhere in my life. (*Powdering her face*) I'd like
to use your phone, P.M. My story is going to be worth a bit to the
Sunday papers.

Sykes March.

*Mrs Pettingal saunters out to the P.M.'s room. Sykes closes the door and
then goes smartly out by the main door*

Appleyard You know, we're getting jolly short of ministers. That's the
Foreign Secretary gone.

Erskine-Pym Well, we shall have to ask Russia and the other countries
to keep quiet for a bit.

Teach I dare say at a pinch I could combine that with my job.

Erskine-Pym Your job at the moment is to get yourself out of the mess
you're in.

Hammer Then there's the War Minister . . .

Erskine-Pym We won't do anything until we've drawn her out. Don't let
her think we suspect her. In the meantime, Hammer, how do you fancy
taking over the War Office?

Hammer Suits me. Give me the army to play with and I'll show you fire-
works . . .

Erskine-Pym Thank you, but I'm not thinking of a Torchlight Tattoo. On
second thoughts, I think the army will be safer with me.

Teach I don't know much about military matters, but I'll have a go.

Erskine-Pym You'll have a rest—you need it.

*Mrs Wittlesham comes in through the main door. She is attractively
dressed and carries a bouquet*

Wittlesham Good evening, all.

Erskine-Pym (*sweetly*) Ah, good evening, Witty. Having a good time?

Wittlesham Oh, a wonderful time. But am I tired!

Erskine-Pym Come and tell us all about it. Get her a drink. There's a
drop of sherry in my room. That'll buck her up.

Teach It'll put her out—it did me.

Wittlesham Nothing to drink, please! I've had so much champagne today
I couldn't look at anything else.

Hammer H'm, quite a beano, eh?

Wittlesham My dear, that's putting it mildly. Oh, and naughty Miss
Teach! I heard all about her little escapade at the B.B.C. Put a cat
among the pigeons, hasn't she? (*She sits in an armchair*)

Hammer Talking of cats, tell us about "Pussy".

Wittlesham "Pussy?" That's me. How did you guess?

Hammer Sort of nickname, eh?

Wittlesham (*giggling*) Yes. Rather silly perhaps, but you know how it is.

Hammer I do not know how it is.

Erskine-Pym I think it's a very pretty name. (*Wagging a playful finger*) And who calls you "Pussy"?

Wittlesham (*coquettishly*) Ah, that's telling. Well, as a matter of fact, it's "Bambi". You don't mind, do you. I know you don't really like Cabinet Ministers having men friends, but . . .

Erskine-Pym Oh, "Bambi's" different. We don't mind "Bambi", do we? You must ask him round sometime.

Wittlesham That is nice of you. I thought you'd be annoyed, but you're taking it so well. And "Bambi" is quite a darling . . .

Hammer Look, has he got another name, or does he run around on four legs?

Wittlesham Oh, no, only two . . .

Sykes bursts in by the main door and goes over to Mrs Wittlesham

Sykes I arrest you . . .

Erskine-Pym Of course, you would muck it up! Just as we were getting her to tell us all she knew.

Sykes Instructions received . . .

Erskine-Pym All right, bob down. (*Grimly*) Now, Mrs Wittlesham, late Minister for War, what have you got to say for yourself?

Wittlesham Oh, anything you like.

Appleyard Do you admit going to cinemas and restaurants with the Leader of the Opposition?

Wittlesham Of course. He is "Bambi".

Hammer She admits it! Conniving with the enemy!

Teach Traitor! And I suppose you've got the army worked up into a state of rebellion?

Wittlesham Oh, no; they're quite happy drilling and marching up and down. And I've been far too busy sewing and getting things together.

Teach Really? Well, the only sewing you're going to do for the next few years will be on mail-bags.

Wittlesham Oh, don't be silly. Mail-bags make such poor material.

Erskine-Pym Remove the prisoner.

Sykes (*tapping Wittlesham on the shoulder*) 'Shun! Left incline. For-ward.

Wittlesham (*rising*) Am I going to prison?

Hammer You are. Probably for life—and even longer.

Wittlesham Well, just for a few minutes, if it amuses you. I can't stay very long, because I've heaps and heaps to do.

Sykes propels Mrs Wittlesham out to the P.M.'s room, then stands by the door

Hammer That's cleared the air a bit. Not a widow left in the Cabinet. And I take it the rest of us are safe?

Erskine-Pym I hope so. But I wish that woman wouldn't stand there. I feel any moment she's going to arrest me.

A band is heard approaching

Now then, Emergency Cabinet Meeting. Take your places.

Mrs Erskine-Pym goes to her usual place at the table. Teach sits on her left and Appleyard next to Teach. Hammer sits on the other side of the P.M.

The question is, what do we do? Any suggestions?

The others look at one another

Well, come on! Don't you realize the country is in dire peril? (*Listening*) What's that?

Appleyard Oh, just part of the mobilization, I expect.

Erskine-Pym (*doubtfully*) Is it? I told you to mobilize the army, not the Dagenham Girl Pipers.

They all listen then move quickly to the windows

Hammer That's no army. They're all women!

Appleyard Well, isn't it the Judo Corps?

Teach No. Look, they're carrying banners.

Erskine-Pym Tell me what they say. I haven't my glasses.

Appleyard (*peering out*) "Give—us—back—our—Men!"

Erskine-Pym Another plot!

Hammer Of course it is. Look who's getting out of that car—the Delisle woman!

Erskine-Pym Coming here?

Hammer Yes, coming here.

Appleyard Right. Action stations. Sykes! Get your man.

Sykes squeezes flat against the wall by the main door. The others crouch behind the table

The door is flung open and Vicki enters, carrying a large suitcase

Sykes leaps forward and claps her on the shoulder

Sykes Don't move!

Vicki (*dropping the case and holding her hands up*) Okay, Sheriff. Guess you've got me.

The others rise from behind the table. Appleyard shuts the door and stands there

Appleyard We've got the master criminal.

Sykes picks up the suitcase

Better be wary of that—probably a bomb in it.

Vicki (*coolly*) Yeah, bomb for you all right. (*Jerking the case away from*

Sykes, she lays it on the table and sits next to it)

Erskine-Pym Make yourself quite comfortable.

Vicki Sure, I will. (*She throws open the suitcase and takes out sheaves of paper*) There you are. Four million signatures demanding your resignation. The rest are in my car outside.

Hammer Resignation!

Vicki (*nodding*) Signed by the housewives of London. We start work on the provinces tomorrow.

Appleyard That's what you think.

Vicki Say, throw in the sponge, girls. You've had it. Look out of that window. Thousands of women with straight hair and not a bit of colour on their faces. All thirsting for your blood.

Appleyard Take her away!

Sykes Prisoner—for-ward! (*She claps Vicki on the shoulder and propels her towards the P.M.'s door*)

Vicki This won't do you any good. In five minutes they'll come in to find out where I am.

Sykes Silence!

Sykes pushes Vicki into the P.M.'s room

Mrs Erskine-Pym goes to the window. The noise has increased a little and there is some cheering

Erskine-Pym I don't like this. Looks to me what you might call a rough house.

Appleyard (*rubbing her hands*) Good. Let 'em all come.

Erskine-Pym You silly creature, this isn't the school hockey match. Do you think I want to be chased round London by a howling mob?

The phone rings

Oh, answer it, do! I bet it's something else beastly.

Teach (*at the phone*) Yes? For you, P.M.

The P.M. takes the receiver and holds it at arm's length

Erskine-Pym Er—yes? . . . What? (*Bellowing*) Well, what do you want! (*Her voice quietens gradually until it becomes mellifluous*) Yes . . . Yes . . . Oh, yes. Yes, of course . . . Oh, yes, yes . . . Yes, dear . . . All right, dear. (*She puts the receiver down slowly*)

Hammer Who was that?

Erskine-Pym (*stunned*) My husband. Arrived back from the Amazon. Says he'll be home to supper—and make it a good one. (*She goes to her chair and flops down*) This is the end.

Teach If you weaken now . . . !

There is a tap at the P.M.'s door

Appleyard Come in. I mean, go back to prison!

Mrs Wittlesham puts her head round the door

Wittlesham May I come in? (*She gently removes Sykes's restraining hand and comes to the table*) I hear you are in a bit of a bother. Maybe I can help you. (*Sitting on the seat next to one to Mrs Hammer*) And you'll never get out of this mess by yourselves. Why don't you settle for a coalition?

Erskine-Pym (*lifting her head from table*) Coalition? Do you think men would listen to that now? They'll just sweep us aside. We're back in the pre-Pankhurst days—finished.

Wittlesham (*calmly*) Oh, dear me, no. And I think I can help you out. You see, I married Mr Cudlip this morning. As the Leader of the Opposition is now my husband, I think I can influence him in the right direction. In fact, I know I can. (*Smiling*) I've been married before.

Hammer (*banging on the table*) No compromise!

Erskine-Pym Oh, dry up. It's a deal! (*She rises*)

The phone rings

Answer that phone. (*Pointing to Sykes*) You! You human stalactite!

Sykes goes to the phone. The others lean over the table arguing with the P.M. The lines are pushed over quickly and overlap

Hammer If you does this . . . !

Appleyard Letting the side down! Letting the side down!

Teach Blackleg! Blackleg!

Appleyard We stand shoulder to shoulder!

Teach Votes for Women!

Sykes comes down from the phone, stands rigid and salutes

Sykes Reporting . . .

Others What?

Sykes Strike of hairdressers over. Appointments may be booked . . .

There is a surge from the table as they move in a body to the phone. They fight for possession of the receiver

Form a queue, please. Form a queue . . .

The door of the P.M.'s room bursts open and all the others join the throng. Sykes shepherds them into line. The noise of the band and cheering swells up, as—

the CURTAIN *falls*

FURNITURE AND PROPERTY LIST

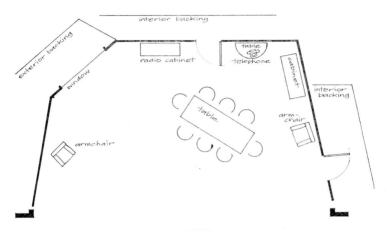

ACT I

On stage: Large table. *On it:* inkwells, blotters, water jugs, glasses, gavel
Radio cabinet. *On it:* vase of flowers
Table. *On it:* telephone, directories, etc.
    Under it: tin of polish, duster
Cabinet. *On it:* vase of flowers. *In drawers:* agenda sheets, notebook
    for **Valerie**, various papers
8 small chairs set as follows: 1 at head of large table, 1 at foot, 3 on
    each side
2 comfortable armchairs
Carpet
Window curtains
On wall above radio: mirror
On wall by main door: bellpush

Off stage: Pile of woman's magazines (**Valerie**)
Parcels and carrier bag containing various items including stockings,
    crochet, 2 paper patterns (**Wittlesham**)
Duster (**Mrs Lurch**)
2 brief-cases stuffed with papers (**Teach**)
Shopping basket, string bag of vegetables (**Hammer**)
Trolley with 8 cups of coffee, saucers, spoons, plate of biscuits
    (**Mrs Lurch**)

Personal **Valerie:** engagement ring
Wittlesham: handkerchief, cigarettes, lighter, watch
Pettingal: powder compact

ACT II

Strike: Papers, etc., from table
              Parcels

Set: Room tidy

Off stage: Letter (**Erskine-Pym**)
              Full brief-case (**Teach**)
              Notebook (**Sykes**)
              Empty brief-case (**Teach**)
              Glass of sherry (**Mrs Lurch**)

Personal: **Wittlesham:** handbag with mirror
              Pettingal: watch
              Vicki: handbag with 2 small parcels and card, watch

ACT III

Off stage: Large wrapped parcel (**Hammer**)
              Beard (**Sykes**)
              Photograph (**Sykes**)
              Notebook (**Valerie**)
              Bouquet (**Wittlesham**)
              Suitcase with papers (**Vicki**)

Personal: **Erskine-Pym:** watch

LIGHTING PLOT

Property fittings required: pendant or wall-brackets
Interior. A Cabinet Room. The same scene throughout

ACT I   Morning

To open: Effect of April sunshine
No cues

ACT II   Evening

To open   Blue exterior. Room in darkness
Cue 1   **Valerie** switches on lights   (Page 19)
              Snap on interior lighting

ACT III   Evening

To open: Room in darkness
Cue 2   **Pettingal** switches on lights   (Page 38)
              Snap on interior lighting

EFFECTS PLOT

ACT I

ACT II

ACT III